Eye on the Hurricane
Eastern Counties

by Bob Ogley and Kev Reynolds

The great storm of October 16, 1987 has already passed into folklore. It was a meteorological event of such magnitude that it will always be one of the great talking points of the late twentieth century. For the inhabitants of Essex, East Anglia and The Fens the wind, which appeared out of nowhere, wreaked havoc. In the early hours of the morning forests were destroyed, aircraft overturned, lorries blown over, cars crushed and roofs and walls sucked from houses and churches. In almost every community from The Thames to The Wash life came to a standstill. This book by Bob Ogley and Kev Reynolds traces the story in photographs and dramatic personal accounts. It also describes how the people of eastern England worked together in adversity and of the energy of gardeners and foresters in planning for the future. It is produced by popular demand as a regional follow-up to the book In The Wake of The Hurricane which was in the top-ten best seller list for eight successive months.

Froglets Publications

Part of the profits from the sale of this book will be donated to naturalists and wildlife trusts in the four counties, of Essex, Suffolk, Norfolk and Cambridgeshire.

First published in Great Britain by
Froglets Publications Limited
Brasted Chart,
Westerham, Kent, TN16 1LY
Telephone (0959 62972) Fax: (0959 65365)

© Bob Ogley and Kev Reynolds 1989

Research by Claire Ogley and Fern Flynn

October 1989 All rights reserved. No part of this publication may be reproduced, stored in a retrieval system, or transmitted in any form or by any other means, electronic, mechanical, photocopying, recording, or otherwise, without the prior permission of the publisher.

ISBN 0 9513019 6 9 (Softcover)
0 9513019 7 7 (Hardcover)

Cover illustrations
Front cover:
The skyline near Tunstall by Nicholas Smith.

Back cover:
Boats beached at Thorpe Bay, 8 am October 16 1987
By Bryan Hervé.

Printed and bound in Great Britain by Staples Printers Rochester Limited, Love Lane, Rochester, Kent, ME1 1TP.

● Special prints of the two cover photographs are available on application to the publishers.

Acknowledgements

DAILY, evening and weekly newspapers in Essex, Cambridge, Suffolk and Norfolk have helped considerably by allowing us to look through their own special storm reports which have served as leads in the preparation of this book. We would like especially to thank the cameramen and women whose professional expertise shines through page after page. In particular we are grateful to the Evening Echo, the Eastern Daily Press, the East Anglian Daily Times, Essex Chronicle series, Essex Gazette, Harlow and Epping Star, the Ipswich Evening Star, Saffron Walden Reporter, Cambridge Evening News, Romford Observer, Lowestoft Journal, Mail Newspapers.

We are also grateful to the witnesses of the storm. Many have been named in the the text but many others have generously spared us time by explaining their involvement and taking us to certain localities. In particular Chris Dunn, Ben Platts-Mills, John Gardiner, Carol Carver, Mary Harvey, Martin Minta, P. Johnston of the Forestry Commission and Janet Millington of the Essex Naturalists' Trust.

County and Borough councils gave great assistance along with The National Trust, the Anglian Weather Centre, the National Meteorological Office, Weather Magazine, the Climatic Research Unit of the University of East Anglia and the Broads Authority. We are especially grateful to Oliver Rackham, research fellow at Corpus Christie College, Cambridge for his valuable contribution and to Mr. Teddy Taylor, M.P..

We are also indebted to the following:
Peter Holborn, Sandra Tricker, Norman Brooks, Pen and Ink Publicity, Lynn Tait Gallery, Epping Forest Conservation Centre, H.M.S.O., S. Bower, Peter Lake, Mick Chubb, D. Squires, Brenda Lambert, D. Standen, G. Shaw, Mr and Mrs Norman Kingston, J. Strauss, Colin Kimble, Colloryan, Paul Kirkby, Bill Clark, Ted Sepple, Charles Stock, Lord Somerleyton, Leslie R. Brand, Stephen Westover, Terry Weeden, David Martin, Adrian Rushton, Ken Clow, N. J. Cotterell, Holly Pelling, Debbie Wolmarans, John Partridge, Martin Freeman, Simon Hodges, H. J. Mothersole, Judy Riggs, Hugh Bostock, Jan Michalak, John Bungay, Brian Bedwell, P. Norman, Ceinwen Thomas, Joyce Middleton, Gordon Anckorn, A. Gregory, Rev. Philip Oliver, Rev. James Cameron, Duncan Morris, David Barker, Chris Riggs, Steve Scott, Charles Hodge, Vernon Place, Audrey Sole, G. R. Mortimer.

A special thanks to Nicholas Smith and Bryan Hervé who took the photographs which we have chosen to feature on the front and back covers respectively.

We huddled together

by Teddy Taylor MP for Southend East who was the first to call for a government inquiry into the lack of warning from weathermen.

THE United Kingdom has frequently suffered from winds strong enough to blow light vessels onto beaches, fell older trees and send chimney pots crashing on the roadways. Such winds, of course, have also devastated crops, causing a cry from farmers that is familiar in all extreme weather conditions—whether it be snow, rain, wind or drought.

But the storm of October 1987 was of an entirely different magnitude. For several hours it was so furious and massive that my family huddled together in one bed, the children believing that something terrible was about to happen. People like us who go to church and enjoy reading the Old Testament appear to have greater visions of possible disaster than those who merely reflect upon the implications of weather forecasts.

Most frightening of all was the moment of real devastation. In our case it was the sickening collapse of two large hunks of masonry on which our chimneys had been built. They crashed through the roof and dust and water poured into the bedroom as the ceiling buckled.

When morning came we saw in our road that the Almighty had not singled us out but houses everywhere had been bruised and battered. Cars had huge dents as crumbling walls had fallen on top of them. The beach at Southend was a jungle of upturned boats and yachts.

The same massive destruction occurred throughout Essex and East Anglia. Parklands had the appearance of war zones in which bombs had fallen, small trees were everywhere in a higgledy-piggledy shambles, roads were blocked and debris strewn across the countryside. So great was the damage that it took months to clear up.

The immediate dangers, such as partly fallen trees, were dealt with by the army and their heavy lifting equipment. Then we had the sudden appearance of breezy men in unstable looking trucks offering to repair our chimneys for cash payments while the more reliable roofing operator worked non-stop, their wives dealing with telephone anxieties and numerous estimates for insurance companies.

The great storm of 1987 was not glamorous or exciting but it was memorable and it was certainly an event which the people of Essex and East Anglia will never forget.

Contents

The wind that changed our landscape

FRIDAY October 16, 1987 is a date that has become indelibly written in the hearts and minds of all who lived through those dark hours of fury as hurricane-force winds lashed sixteen bewildered English counties. It is a date none will forget who saw familiar landscapes rearranged, their homes battered, their prized possessions or businesses flattened and, in some especially harrowing cases, their loved ones killed. In a few brutal hours of darkness the south-east of England became a battleground. Nature's battleground.

Not since 1703 had England experienced anything like the winds that tore across this unsuspecting land. History was proclaimed by the great storm's roar and in the crashing of innumerable trees, roofs, barns, fences and walls. There was a madness abroad, that mid-October morning, and a stunned population could do nothing to calm it.

We are unused to such drama.

Ours is a benevolent land. A land of soft horizons, of productive fields and gentle, welcoming landscapes. Our homes nestle comfortably in the folds of an ancient countryside threatened only by the works of man, for Nature on the whole has been kind to this fair corner of England where her excesses are mostly but minor aggravations. When changes come they occur slowly. We can adapt our minds and our lives to absorb them.

But what happened in the dark hours of that black Friday morning has bred a new and profound sense of respect for the forces of Nature. By comparison, man now sees himself as a creature of feeble means.

The night of Thursday October 15 began innocently enough. True, after long weeks of heavy rain rivers were rising and Grade B flood warnings given. A brash of wind was teasing the trees that were still in full leaf. But in no sense did they hint at what was to come.

The nation went to bed expecting to rise next morning to familiar sights and familiar sounds. Who in the south-east could possibly know that they were closing their eyes on a world that would no longer appear the same again?

Meanwhile a depression had been centering over the Bay of Biscay where at midday pressure stood at 976 mbs. By nightfall pressure was still falling. Western France was enduring heavy winds and by 10.00 pm the southern counties of England were feeling the initial blasts of the rising gale, with gusts of 46 mph being reported inland. Shortly after midnight the Channel Islands took the full force of a raging storm that had stirred itself and was now heading north-east towards southern England. As it did so the winds rose to gusts of more than 100 miles an hour. The Normandy coast experienced blasts of 117 knots—135 mph.

At 3.00 am on Friday pressure had plunged to 957 mbs at the centre of the depression, which was near Bristol and racing northward.

As the wind roared across the southern landscape, so countless terrified families woke in fear to discover trees crashing round their homes, or even on their homes. From the Channel to the Wash the fingers of the hurricane spread their misery and plucked terror at several million hearts.

The worst of the wind to hit London came between 2.00 and 3.00 am; Hampshire, Sussex and Kent were being lashed by devastating 100 mph gusts around 4 o'clock and by six most of the southern counties in a line from the Severn Estuary to the Wash were in no doubt that a major meteorological event was taking place. This was the time when East Anglia was affected most, while in the Midlands wind speeds were of a moderate gale force and blowing at less than 40 mph.

From Dorset to Norfolk the hurricane bulldozed its relentless course, leaving in its wake a trail of heartbreak and devastation. Great swathes of woodland were turned to matchwood. Some fifteen million trees are estimated to have been felled by the wind. Houses, schools, hospitals and hotels all had chimney pots down or roofs lifted and torn away.

Electricity pylons fell like skittles, sending high-voltage cables writhing and arcing through the night like lightning as though from a violent electrical storm. The National Grid failed. Greenhouses shed their glass over acres of neighbourhood gardens. Grounded aircraft were overturned on several exposed airfields. Two firemen died in Dorset when a tree crashed onto their fire engine answering what turned out to be a false alarm. At Hastings a fisherman was killed when he was hit by a flying beach hut. Boats were tossed ashore and destroyed. A cross-channel ferry was thrown onto the rocks at Folkestone. At Southend the wind was so powerful it held back the tide and boat owners going to inspect the damage found they could walk across the mud as far as the pier-head at high tide, and in the mouth of the River Crouch, Essex Marina, with its landing stage and craft attached, broke free of its pier foundations and was blown across to Burnham.

Yet amazingly, miraculously, the death toll was comparatively small and whilst nineteen people tragically lost their lives as a direct result of the storm, that figure might have been so much higher.

As it was, when the grey light of dawn filtered night away, bewildered villagers and townsfolk alike across a large belt of south-east England found that their homes had no power, no telephone and, in many instances no water either.

And the landscape had changed.

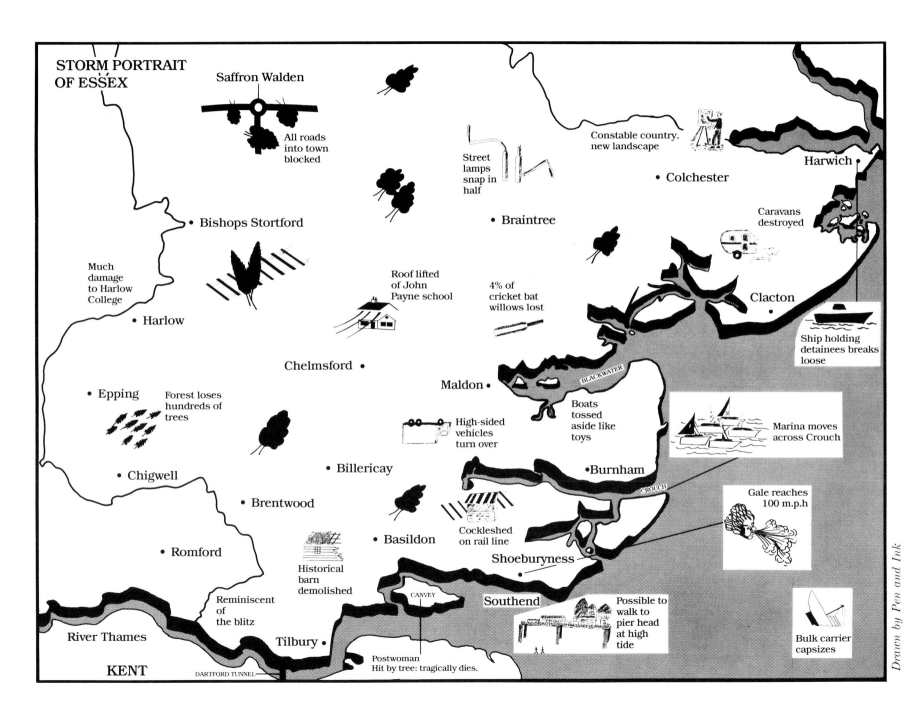

STORM PORTRAIT OF ESSEX

Saffron Walden
All roads into town blocked

Constable country, new landscape

Harwich

Street lamps snap in half

Colchester

Caravans destroyed

Braintree

Clacton

Bishops Stortford

Much damage to Harlow College

Roof lifted of John Payne school

4% of cricket bat willows lost

Ship holding detainees breaks loose

Harlow

Chelmsford

Maldon

BLACKWATER

Boats tossed aside like toys

Epping

Forest loses hundreds of trees

High-sided vehicles turn over

Marina moves across Crouch

Billericay

Burnham

CROUCH

Chigwell

Gale reaches 100 m.p.h

Brentwood

Cockleshed on rail line

Shoeburyness

Romford

Basildon

Historical barn demolished

Reminiscent of the blitz

CANVEY

Southend

Possible to walk to pier head at high tide

Bulk carrier capsizes

River Thames

Tilbury

KENT

DARTFORD TUNNEL

Postwoman Hit by tree: tragically dies.

Drawn by Pen and Ink

5

Essex in the Hurricane

ESSEX is not a county of epics. Since the war its agriculture has seen many changes, but then so have most English counties. Woods have been cut down, hedgerows grubbed out. Mechanised agri-business has taken the place of small farms that once employed half a village, and today's traveller is as likely to see vast prairies of oil-seed rape as traditional fields of waving corn, on his journey from one side of the county to the other.

Major roads sprout like bindweed almost everywhere. Villages have grown into dormitory towns and towns spread one against another until they are virtually absorbed into one great conurbation.

It's a county of commuters. A county on the move. A county of cars and housing estates, of bustle and industry. Sometimes one can almost believe there is an official determination to cover the Essex countryside in concrete and brick.

But this is only one side of the picture.

Turn away from the A-class roads, and the B-class roads too, and you will find another Essex. This is a land of winding lanes and flower-filled ditches, of footpaths that lead into a secretive countryside inhabited by fox and rabbit, stoat and weasel. Pink-walled cottages stand uneven beneath a pair of oaks; rooks circle over clusters of thatch; a black timbered barn leans against the breeze, a windmill signals with white sails from one low hill to the next. There are herds of fallow deer stepping lightly on the woodland fringe while peewits wheel and cry from ploughed fields of autumn and nightingales trill in the calm of twilight. Owls haunt farmyards lost to the madding crowd.

Essex wears two faces. But neither is accustomed to dramas of epic proportions.

In September 1958 the Essex Naturalists' Trust was formed. An invitation to the first meeting bore the statement. "The countryside of our county is changing rapidly." How true that statement was! But not as true as it might have been had it been written in October 1987.

In the worst winds to hit southern England in almost 300 years, Essex took a battering. From Epping to Harwich and from Southend to Harlow the hurricane played skittles across an unsuspecting and vulnerable landscape. It made no difference whether that landscape was dominated by residential streets or undulating fields and woodlands. The game was the same. Only it wasn't a game that the people of Essex could appreciate.

A trail of destruction littered the county. Trees thumped onto roads alongside Epping Forest. They brought down power cables, and fell upon houses, sheds and garages throughout Essex. British Rail's Eastern Region had to clear about 2,000 trees and a Leigh-on-Sea cockle shed from its lines before it could resume a normal service. The Central Line of the London Underground that runs above ground between Epping and Ongar was out of action for three days after sixty trees blocked the line.

Billericay itself was virtually cut off, and at Wickford a falling tree tangled in overhead wires crashed through the bedroom window of Mrs Jean Smith. Neither Mrs Smith nor her family were hurt.

Dozens of Essex schools suffered too; mostly with roofing problems. St John Payne in Chelmsford was probably the worst hit, but others suffered in a swathe encompassing Harwich, Rainham, Romford and Havering. Romford Ice Rink lost it roof, as did a block of flats on the Limes Farm Estate, Chigwell. Debris landed on five cars and demolished two garden walls.

In Loughton David and Gill Barrett slept on as the hurricane tore at the roof of their flat in Avondale Close. They were woken at 4.00 am by the telephone when a cousin living nearby phoned to say their roof had fallen off. Mr Barrett looked out of the window and felt ill. "I thought it was something out of *Poltergeist*," he said.

All along the East Coast from Southend to Harwich the storm roared its fury, smashing seafront properties and tossing boats onto land. But as light came to the day, adding visible evidence to overnight misery, the wild seas proved too tempting for sailboard enthusiasts who braved 70 mph winds to pursue their sport.

In company with numerous other parts of Essex the Brentwood district lost a good many trees, and Thriftwood, the 73 acre Scout camping ground at Ingrave, was badly hit. Fortunately there were no Scouts camping there at the time. Forestry workers from Leeds and Wellingborough were drafted in to help with the task of clearing storm-damaged woodlands around Brentwood.

In the north of the county all roads into Saffron Walden were blocked by fallen trees and the police called upon the army to help tackle the chaos. Men from the 9/12th Royal Lancers at Carver Barracks, Wimbish, answered the call with axes, saws and recovery vehicles. "We enjoyed doing it," said Major James Short who was in charge of the operation.

In Wimbish itself a huge lime tree just missed the White Hart pub when it came crashing down, bringing with it power lines and plunging the whole area into darkness for three days. Mr James Jones, the pub's landlord, found enough candles to enable him to pull pints with his wife Patricia until the power was restored.

Life, after all, had to go on. The hurricane may have ploughed many a scar on the Essex landscape, and its effects would be felt for a very long time. But as soon as the winds had died down, October 16 1987 became part of history. A history worth recording.

Southend Battered

FROM Leigh to Shoeburyness, Southend has seven miles of south-facing foreshore—and no protection at all from the savage winds of Black Friday.

The town took a battering as the wind lashed across the water with such force that it held back the tide. Boats were hurled out of the water to end up splintered on the seafront or even on the road, and scores of beach huts disintegrated to matchwood. All along the seafront, cafes and amusement arcades lost their windows, and long strings of illuminations were dashed to the ground. Roofs of flats on the eastern promenade were ripped open to the elements, bringing heartbreak, fear and confusion to the occupants.

Two huge plate glass windows blew in at Keddie's store and security guards were on duty at 4.30 in the morning to protect valuable merchandise from looters. Outside the pavement was strewn with tangled aluminium slats torn from the store's frontage. "It is the worst damage I have ever seen," said store manager, Mr Carl Maufe "But it will be business as usual."

A 16-pot chimney crashed through the roof of the nearby Railway Hotel and landed in the bedroom of Sarah Barrett, the licensee's daughter who was luckily away visiting friends at the time. The roof, function room and public bar were all badly damaged.

The intensive care unit at Southend Hospital was put out of action when the windows were smashed by the winds, and for a time it was necessary to close operating theatres. Out at the town's airport a huge hangar collapsed, wrecking the aircraft kept inside, while light planes parked out on the airfield were completely tossed over, causing thousands of pounds' worth of damage.

Essex Radio presenter, Romilly Paradine, had a nightmare journey from her home in Leigh to the studios in the centre of Southend. "Trees lay across the road," she said. "Cables were dangling. Bushes, milk bottles and rubbish sacks were blowing about. There was even a complete set of garden furniture lying in the road.

"Suddenly, turning a corner, to my astonishment I came across a milkman making his rounds despite the storm."

Leigh itself took a beating. In Fleming Avenue concrete roof supports from an adjacent car showroom collapsed onto the bungalow of Michael Hogg. Mr Hogg escaped with just a bump on his head—and a headache of a problem as he took stock of the damage to his home.

Firemen were called to Marine Avenue to rescue Stephen Coombs who had climbed onto the roof of his parents' home to steady a wind-loosened chimney, and then found himself trapped there.

Photograph by Evening Echo, Basildon

A battered beach hut on Southend's eastern foreshore.

For those in peril on the sea

RED flares were sighted off the Isle of Grain between the Thames and Medway Estuaries in the early morning of the hurricane. Coxswain Robin Castle and his crew of Waveney class lifeboat, *Helen Turnbull*, put to sea from a safe berth in Sheerness harbour in answer to the distress signal and almost immediately found themselves pitching and rolling in a violent sea. All safety lines were rigged and life-jacket lights activated in anticipation of a difficult and hazardous mission in those appalling conditions.

The wind was gusting above 90 knots (104 mph) and breaking seas of 20 to 25 feet gave the crew of the 44 ft lifeboat a very rough ride. Spray, spume and frequent squalls of rain reduced visibility almost to zero. Navigation was possible only by radar, and when Second Coxswain Dennis Bailey was thrown heavily against the instrument as the lifeboat rolled more than seventy degrees, it was some moments before the radar trace could be regained. Echo sounders gave erratic readings because of the violent motion.

Grain Coastguard had reported the sighting of a small angling boat with two people aboard, and at 7.17 am a red flare was sighted by the lifeboat crew off Allhallows.

Coxswain Castle edged the *Helen Turnbull* with the utmost caution through increasingly shallow water towards the casualty. Because of the direction of wind and ebbing tide it was impossible to float the small inflatable. Neither would a rocket line reach the casualty in the storm,

and as the anglers' boat was being swamped over its gunwales and slowly sinking, there was no alternative but to take the lifeboat as close as possible and lift the anglers off.

The lifeboat crew tried using a loud hailer to instruct the anglers to cut their anchor, but they were unable to make themselves heard above the roar of the wind and shrieking seas.

By the time their instructions were finally heard, the lifeboat was almost alongside and the two survivors hauled aboard, taken below and strapped in for safety.

As she manoeuvred clear the *Helen Turnbull* was caught by a strong gust which suddenly swung the lifeboat's bow to starboard, and the stern ran aground. For half an hour Coxswain Castle and his crew tried in vain to free her. Then Second Coxswain Bailey and Crew Member Richard Rogers volunteered to go overboard to float a spare anchor seaward to pull the lifeboat clear. This brave effort also failed and with the lifeboat settling on an even keel, the struggle to free her was abandoned as the tide receded. It was not until the next high tide, eleven hours later, that the *Helen Turnbull* was refloated, fortunately without having sustained any damage.

Thirteen hours after setting out in the hurricane's fury, the *Helen Turnbull* was returned safely to Sheerness.

For their part in the rescue Coxswain Robin Castle was awarded the RNLI's bronze medal for bravery. Second Coxswain Dennis Bailey and Crew Member Richard Rogers were awarded the thanks of the RNLI inscribed on vellum, and Crew Members Peter Bullin, Eamonn French and Brian Spoor awarded bronze medal certificates.

Photographs by Colin Nicholson

Helen Turnbull—a hazardous mission in appalling conditions.

Coxswain Robin Castle.

'Your store has fallen down'

THE hurricane had no respect for old or new. Ancient buildings and recent constructions were treated alike with scorn. Business premises, private homes, hospitals and schools all bore their share of the devastation. Whatever lay in the path of that vicious wind was fair game.

For weeks Joe Strauss and his sons had worked to prepare new premises for their decorating supplies business, S and A Supplies, on the corner of Milton Road and London Road, Westcliff. The shop was due to open on Saturday October 17th.

But a telephone call in the early hours of Friday the 16th led to a sudden change of plan. 'Your store has fallen down,' Mr Strauss was told.

It had, too. It looked as though a bomb had exploded. The roof had gone, and the Milton Road side of the shop was blown out. Glass, bricks, metal and timber debris lay strewn over the pavement and across the road. The road was blocked and decorating supplies were exposed to the elements.

'We worked from six in the morning until eight that night without a break,' said Mr Strauss's son, explaining how they'd attempted to make the building safe and clear as much stock as they could. 'It was the hardest day's work we'd ever done.'

The double-frontage decorating store in Westcliff's busy London Road now has a pristine, sturdy appearance. It took a full year to rebuild, but for Joe Strauss, his sons and many others throughout the southeast, it will take more than new bricks and mortar to erase the memory of that wild night and the hectic day's work that followed.

Photograph by Lyn Tait Gallery

The scene at the junction of Milton Road and London Road, Westcliff as the dust settled on the worst storm in living memory.

Photograph by Kev Reynolds

*The double frontage decorating store today.
It took a full year to rebuild.*

A chimney rests precariously on a roof at Marine Parade, Leigh.

Another chimney—but this one is on top of Magboul Choudry's car at London Road, Hadleigh.

A tree lies against a house in The Ridgeway, Westcliff. Another rests on the garden wall, just missing the family car.

This tumbledown view of Epping Forest, taken immediately after the storm, tells a story of sadness, devastation and possible neglect. Nothing is further from the truth. Epping received minimal damage, because of the sheltering effect and the fact that the trees were not in an advanced state of decay. In the more public areas many of the fallen trees have been cleared and there is a patchwork of new growth produced by windblown and birdsown seeds. Foxgloves and willowherb are competing with birch and rowan, encouraged perhaps by the more mature beech and hornbeam. Epping, all 6,500 acres of it, has the hallmarks of a medieval forest that is alive, well and, to the delight of the Epping Forest Conservation Centre, thriving.

11

Drama of The Jagged Curve

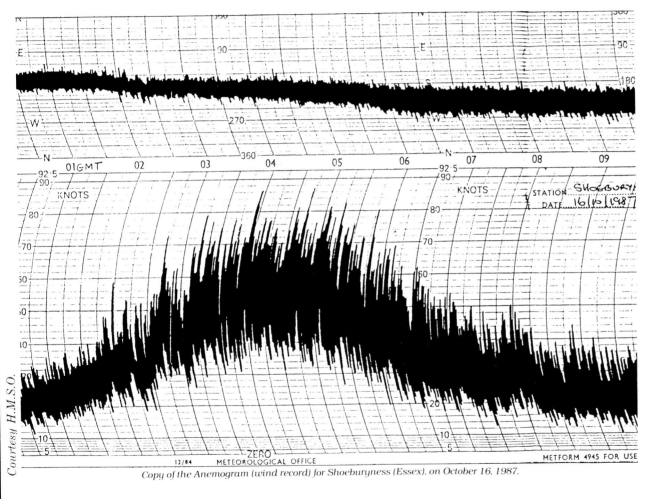

Copy of the Anemogram (wind record) for Shoeburyness (Essex), on October 16, 1987.

Courtesy H.M.S.O.

THE weather observation station at Shoeburyness traced out this jagged curve on its wind meter. It shows the strength, in knots, of the wind and the increasingly wild transition between the gusts and the lulls.

It was at 3 am that the severity of the storm was becoming apparent. By then the depression was centred over the Somerset Levels and gusts in the south-east were exceeding 80 knots. At 2.50 am the London Weather Centre recorded 82 knots–higher than any other reading for central London since records began.

At Shoeburyness the first gust in excess of 60 knots occurred just before 3 am. This is clearly shown on the anemograph trace. For the next 2½ hours the wind on this south-facing Essex coastline scarcely dropped below 60 knots—violent Storm Force 11 on the Beaufort Scale.

The highest gust speed at Shoeburyness was at 4.50 am when 87 knots was recorded–exactly 100 miles an hour and a speed unlikely to return for 500 years.

In southern Essex the storm was at its worst between 4 am and 5 am. At 5 am the depression was centred between Leicester and Peterborough and the occlusion was swinging rapidly across southern England, its passage being marked by a sharp fall in temperature and an astounding rise in pressure.

The upper line of this anemograph shows the direction of the wind.

This True-Craft lorry from Leeds was blown over near the Kursaal in Southend and all along the promenade strings of bulbs trail on the ground.

13

A tale of two chimneys

TWO scenes that typify the morning after the storm and the topsy-turvy few days that followed. A chimney rests precariously against the roof of the house next door at Leigh Hill, Leigh and firemen nearby remove a chimney stack, brick by brick.

The battle to open the wilderness, remove trees which were leaning on houses, take away dangerously hanging masonry and beams was not without its real dangers. (On that first morning parts of Essex appeared to be bomb-damaged and it was fortunate that no-one was killed.)

Firemen across south east Essex were inundated with calls for help. For roof repairers and builders the storm brought an unprecedented volume of work.

The damage prompted insurance companies in Essex and East Anglia to open special claims offices. The payout was the biggest in their history and most customers were delighted with the way the companies rose to the occasion.

Photographs by Evening Echo, Basildon

Photograph by Evening Echo, Basildon

Fallen trees block Woodgrange Drive, Thorpe Bay. How well local residents remember this scene.

Photograph by Brian T. Ellingford

The roof of this house in Chalkwell Avenue, Chalkwell was blown away in the night. The upper storey of this house has now been transformed with two front facing dormer windows and a side dormer.

Wind held back the tide

AS the wind hurtled across the Thames Estuary it came face to face with the busy Essex coastline where long lines of small boats and fishing vessels bobbed up and down in their customary sleeping place.

They were rudely awakened; in fact so powerful was the wind that the oncoming tide was held back and boats from Canvey to Shoebury and beyond were blown over into the mud.

Bryan Herve's magnificent photograph on the back cover captures the scene at Thorpe Bay where 22 boats were left stranded. On the Friday morning local people organised a JCB to pull the boats upright and on the evening tide, with the wind still blowing, Bryan carefully towed each of them back to sea.

Sadly there were casualties. Three boats were smashed by the wind and had to be left behind but 19 survived and by Saturday were back in a more gentle sea.

History— in a heap

Photograph by Evening Echo, Basildon

GREAT Wheatley Farm stands on an exposed hillside to the west of Rayleigh, gazing over low-lying land towards Basildon. To the side of the farmhouse stands a black-timbered barn that must have withstood quite a few gales in its 300 year history.

However in the hurricane of October 1987 it shivered and groaned under the onslaught of some of the fiercest winds ever known in England. Those winds hurtled across that low-lying land, skimmed up the hillslope, lopped the tops off some of farmer Norman Kingston's apple trees and hammered at the lofty timber building. Part of the hundred-foot long barn was demolished, as our picture shows, but remarkably the remainder, twisted and weakened though it was, refused to go down.

Two years on remnants of this 17th century listed barn were still standing exposed and vulnerable. Mr Kingston had plans to restore the building, but since the needs of modern farming are quite different to those of 300 years ago, he now intends to reduce it to half its original length. The wind, of course, has already made a start.

The dreadful aftermath. The stark view of Essex University, Colchester, showing four of the residential towers and the sports centre; the roofs of some student quarters were damaged and the windows smashed but no one was hurt.

THIS photograph by Evening Echo cameraman, Maurice Edwards was chosen for the front page of a marvellous souvenir supplement published just after the storm. It not only depicts the kind of despair which faced hundreds of families in Essex that morning but also the great resolve of the British people to get on with the job. Forget the immediate grief; there's work to be done—strenuous outdoor work for the whole family. This badly damaged home belongs to Bradley and Rosemary Russell of Church Road, Rayleigh. Will they ever forget the moment this picture was taken?

The Hockley craftsmen

MILLIONS of trees were uprooted, crowns snapped off, and great limbs torn from lofty trunks and thrown to the ground in woods, parks and on farmland all over the south-east. For weeks and months after the storm tree surgeons and timber merchants alike were inundated with cries for help.

In Hockley Woods, near Rochford, the largest and most varied ancient wood in Essex, acres of sweet chestnut which should have been coppiced twenty years earlier, were blown over. Valleys of hornbeam were levelled and some magnificent large oaks crashed under the channelled force of the wind.

Much of the sweet chestnut has since been cleared, but some of the hornbeam, having little commercial value, may never be touched. However the rotting timber will attract a wide range of insects and become a natural home for wildlife, while a novel use has been found for some of the oakwood by pioneering British woodworkers, Jim Partridge and Liz Walmsley in a project jointly funded by the Countryside Commission, and the Rochford and Castle Point District Councils, with additional support from Common Ground and Eastern Arts.

"New uses need to be found for woodland timber to safeguard the future of small woods up and down the country," said Brian Watmough, the South-East Essex Woodland Project Officer who commissioned the work, "and we hope that this successful project will inspire others to explore the possibilities."

In three months during the winter of 1988/89 Jim and Liz created a number of items that are both functional and attractive. Using the branches of two of the largest oaks to fall, they have made impressive archways. They have also created a pond-side jetty with stepping stones.

On the eastern extremity of Hockley Woods, the small pond—with its water violets and both smooth and palmate newts, its frogs and toads and marshy fringe dominated by many plants including ragged robin, stitchwort and water mint—is popular with local school parties undertaking environmental studies. The jetty, carved from storm-blown sweet chestnut and hatched with diamond grid patterns to prevent slipping, gives a viewing platform without damaging the banks of the pond. The stepping stones are a mixture of oak and sweet chestnut logs.

These splendid innovations are a testimony of modern craftmanship that should serve as a stimulus for others. They are expected to survive for at least fifty years, by which time seedlings of the original hurricane-levelled trees will be well on their way to maturity to bring continuing pleasure to generations for whom October 16 1987 will be a date of little significance.

Photograph by Kev Reynolds

Spring in Hockley Woods—a testimony of modern craftmanship.

One of two archways, reminiscent of Icelandic whale-bone work, created by Jim Partridge from a single piece of storm blown timber.

Photographs: Before: B. O. Sewell, D. Constance Ltd. After: Peter Lake Task Force Trees.

Before and After . . . The beautiful setting of All Saints' Church, Brightlingsea was wiped out. Task Force Trees, a special unit of the Countryside Commission tackling the storm damage to trees, helped with the replanting.

and between . . . Furious activity to clear the stricken churchyard at All Saints, Brightlingsea captured in Mick Chubb's evocative picture.

Dirty work

BASILDON Hospital Manager, Mr Geoff Shaw, was called out at 5.30 in the morning, given a hard hat to wear and shown the roof of the hospital laundry. It's a flat-topped pyramid and both ends had been blown out by the hurricane. Debris from the roof had showered onto machinery below, and the roof itself was swaying in the tempest.

Until engineers could satisfy Mr Shaw that the roof was not about to collapse, laundry workers were sent home, but emergency stabilising repairs were carried out and the laundry was back in full production within a week of the hurricane—although without a full roof over the workers' heads.

Total cost of replacing the damaged roof and broken windows elsewhere in the hospital came to £40,000, all of which was met by the Regional Health Authority, much to Mr Shaw's relief.

Photographs by Evening Echo, Basildon

The roof of Allders warehouse in Paycocke Road, Basildon was blown away and stock inside ruined by the wind. To add insult to injury water sprinklers came on and added to the damage. David James, merchandise manager surveys the scene.

A leafy archway for the horseriders in Birch Grove, Wickford. The tree did not survive.

Photograph: Essex Chronicle Series

Bring Back the Horses

Naturalists' Trusts and The Nature Conservancy Council are anxious to point out how much can be gained for the environment by allowing natural regrowth wherever possible; this will enrich habitats instead of destroying them. Here we see the ideal way to clear fallen wood with the minimum damage to the woodland floor. A Suffolk Punch at a demonstration day in High Woods May 1988.

Photograph by Essex Naturalists' Trust, Edward Clack

Copperas Wood one of Essex's most badly hit woodlands on the Stour Estuary near Harwich. A site of special scientific interest as is nearby Stour Wood, the Essex Naturalists' Trust owns 34½ acres of which 20-25 acres were flattened. A special non-intervention area of about 4 acres—in the centre foreground—is being monitored.

Photograph by A. Gregory, Harlow Star

Six poplars came down in the grounds of Norway House, North Weald, the former RAF station building and now a council home for the homeless.

The Beaufort Scale of wind velocity

Sir Francis Beaufort (1774-1857) was an English admiral who gave his name to an international scale of wind velocities ranging from 0 (calm) to 12 (hurricane). The table shown below helps add perspective to the events of October 16 1987.

No on Scale	Wind Description	General Effects	Velocity MPH
0	Calm	Smoke rises vertically	0
1	Light air movement	Direction indicated by smoke; wind vanes unaffected	2
2	Light breeze	Breeze felt on face; leaves rustle; wind vanes move	5
3	Gentle breeze	Leaves & small twigs in motion; light flags extended	10
4	Moderate breeze	Small branches move; dust and paper rise	15
5	Fresh breeze	Small trees in leaf sway; crested wavelets on inland water	21
6	Strong breeze	Larger branches in motion; telegraph wires whistle	27
7	Moderate gale	Whole trees in motion; walking inconvenient	35
8	Fresh gale	Twigs break off; walking impeded	42
9	Strong gale	Slight structural damage	50
10	Whole gale	Trees uprooted; structural damage	59
11	Storm	Wide-spread damage	69
12	Hurricane	Wide-spread damage	75
	Violent hurricane	Wide-spread damage	100

It looks like crumpled cardboard. In fact it's the roof from Harlow College's east site which was mangled by the wind. The library was closed, books were removed and the students' refectory also closed.

Angry-morning. The view from Barrack Lane, Dovercourt across to Felixstowe 8 a.m. 16.10.87.

Not Birnam Wood to Dunsinane, but just as strange an occurrence when the Essex Marina at Wallasea broke loose from its concrete piers and was swept across the Crouch to Burnam with 60 boats in tow. Many small craft were lost.

Photograph by Paul Kirkby

Residents of St John's Avenue, Old Harlow are looking at the uprooted tree with some anxiety. It has fallen on the roof just above the bedroom of 71-year-old Marjorie Shipton. Marjorie was hurt but it was nothing to do with the tree. She had broken her foot and was sleeping downstairs oblivious to the drama outside. If that was one lucky 'break' then there was an even better one in store for the pensioner. Neighbour Paul Kirkby who took this picture befriended Marjorie and now invites her to spend Christmas with him and his family.

Photograph by A. Gregory, Harlow Star

A surburban scene, typical of many Essex towns, on that never-to-be-forgotten morning. With a casual glance at the destruction a lady from Chippingfield walks her dogs in Wayre Street, Old Harlow.

Wandlebury beeches in the Gog Magog Hills near Cambridge before and after the trauma. We see the same tree in the right foreground of the before picture (left) and in the right background of the post-October 16th 1987 picture, which also shows Wendy Clark, the wife of warden Bill, with their dog Fagus, meaning beech. The same battered tree can be seen in the 1989 picture of Bill Clark on page 56.

32

Photograph by Ted Sepple, Romford Observer

Heath Park Engineering Company in Brentwood Road, Romford–four vehicles-in a single blow!

Southend Airport on the morning of October 16, 1987. A hangar had collapsed in the night and planes were damaged. Miraculously the airport was still operational.

Owner of Stapleford Flying Club, John Chicken, watched helplessly as the wind tore this TB9 from its mooring straps, lifted it into the air and flipped it onto its back. Other aircraft were shuffled together but without major damage.

The scene at Pemberton Avenue, Gidea Park, Romford which was poignantly described by John Hill of the Romford Observer. "On what had seemed just another autumn night, the savage elements swept across surburbia in all their fury, reminding us with unspeakable ferocity that there is always a wild world outside the cosy confines of our cities ... The trees brought home the stark truth that, on earth at least, nothing is forever."

Photographs by Ted Sepple, Romford Observer

Scaffolding poles replaced people in Romford's usually bustling Market Place.

*Another bungalow, another tree, another nightmare and another insurance claim.
This is Upminster.*

Homes bordering the historic Norsey Wood, Billericay were showered with debris during the storm. From the air this was the scene of despair. Today the beneficial effects are apparent.

From despair to hope

Warden Nigel Wood looks dazed and shaken in the wilderness of Norsey Wood. There is more light today, more wild flowers and wildlife has increased.

THE extensive recreation area of historic Norsey Wood at Billericay was badly hit, as our photograph clearly shows. Among the casualties was a sweet chestnut said to be 300 years old and reputed to have served as a gallows for many years.

Warden, Nigel Wood, was understandably dazed and shaken by his discovery of the wilderness that overnight replaced the glory of this popular and much-loved woodland. Mr Wood's assistant, Paul Joslin, told reporters at the time that there was so much work to be done to make the wood safe, that it would have to be closed to the public indefinitely. Damage was not restricted to the inner wood, but neighbouring properties were also threatened by dangerous trees along the boundary. The main priority then was to clear access and make the wood safe, and to remove those trees that were a danger to properties.

However, as Basildon's Countryside Officer Dave Standen now reports, initial reactions proved overly pessimistic, and as many woodland owners have since discovered, there were to be beneficial side effects to the hurricane.

Prior to October 1987 Norsey Wood consisted mostly of overmature chestnut coppice, and the wind helped clear some of this timber. Added light has produced more wild flowers over a larger area, and it is thought that wildlife there has increased. Two years after the storm remote parts of the wood still have restricted access, and this too has meant some wildlife species are left undisturbed.

Experiments are under way to see how windblown trees react to being reseated, while a third of all those felled by the hurricane are being left for possible re-seeding. "It's possible," said Mr Standen, "that we'll be able to re-plant from self-sown saplings. And I should think that within five years the coppice cycle will be restored and reinstated."

From despair to optimism is but a short stroll through Norsey Wood.

Photograph by Essex Chronicle Series

The B1007 near Stock Church was completely cut off and bulldozers were used to clear the fallen trees. At St. Andrew's Hospital Staff spent many hours checking power cables in Stock Road after large trees had fallen on to them.

Photograph by Fern Flynn

The B1007 at the same spot today.

Riding out the storm

Tossed aside like toys. A photograph by Charles Stock after his great adventure.

CHARLES Stock of Chelmsford is a marine photographer with a passion for sailing. In his little green gaff cutter *Shoal Waters* he has sailed more than 38,000 sea miles around the East Coast over the past twenty-five years, and when the hurricane winds woke him that eventful morning he was anxious to be with her in her hour of greatest need. She was riding her mooring twelve miles away at Heybridge and with high tide imminent she would soon be flung helplessly by the wind and the surf—would her mooring hold?

As he went to his garage a cascade of roof tiles fell on his neighbour's car, and on the road to Great Baddow branches from swaying roadside trees littered the way ahead. Dodging fallen trees and live electricity cables that danced with sparks he drove a slalom course to Danbury, only to find the main road completely blocked. A nifty diversion through a housing estate brought him back on the Maldon road, but just outside Maldon itself a large tree lay prostrate in his path. Luckily it was opposite a garage which gave him the opportunity to swing round it. Yet it was floods, not fallen trees, that finally halted further progress only half a mile from Heybridge. In water boots he waded across fields to the sea-wall, being almost knocked over by the wind.

And there she was,, riding the frantic surf. *Shoal Waters.*

In a moment's desperation Mr Stock stripped to his underpants and half-swam, half-waded through the surf that rolled over his head—and at last hauled himself aboard his wildly pitching little boat. The main hatch had gone, but all else appeared to be sound—although a white cruiser having broken its mooring was bearing down on her and would cause considerable damage if it couldn't be deflected. She was fended off, but another raced up, bounced past and sank.

A makeshift canopy was fitted over the cockpit and a cup of tea brewed down below while *Shoal Waters* pitched and tossed in the teeth of the storm.

Gradually light streaked the sky, the tide fell and the surf eased. As Mr Stock waded ashore the full impact of the hurricane on Heybridge Basin and Mill Beach became evident. Most of the larger boats had gone. Many of the smaller vessels that had stayed their moorings had been damaged by others, like the white cruiser, that had broken theirs. Masts protruded from the water and along Mill Beach around 40 boats lay in distress, while windblown debris was scattered across the marshes.

For Charles Stock there was a great sense of exhilaration mixed with a secret tinge of shame for having enjoyed so much the night he rode the storm.

Imagine the bewilderment of boat owners who arrived at the Essex Marina on the morning of the storm to check their craft, only to find that the marina itself was missing. Such was the strength of the wind that the Cargo landing stage was pulled away from its moorings at Wallasea and swept across the River Crouch. In tow a plethora of small boats were tossed and turned by the heaving tide. Some capsized but were dragged along with their companions to the mud banks near Burnham-on-Crouch. This was the scene when some owners at last located their craft.

Photograph by Leslie R. Brand

The tragic scene at Spring Elms Farm, Little Baddow.

Photograph by Essex Chronicle Series

Nick Saunders of Great Baddow and the limbs of the great cedar which smashed builders' huts and a garage.

Hell in the hen house

THE savage winds tore a swathe through Spring Elms Farm, Little Baddow, leaving poultry farmer Michael Lambert and his wife Brenda wondering how they would cope.

Their farmhouse was virtually untouched, but there was a scene of total chaos where once stood the chicken sheds housing thousands of birds. Two of the sheds were completely demolished; others had shifted on their bases, one having taken a 500 gallon oil drum with it. Fibre glass insulation was strewn over hedges, in trees and across the nearby road. Half the roof of one of the sheds had been ripped off and was nowhere to be seen. It was later found half a mile away, having flown across a road and over the tops of several houses.

About 1,500 chickens had been crushed when their shed collapsed on them, but with the ready support of neighbours ("They were fantastic," said Mrs Lambert) thousands of survivors were rounded up, put in crates and transferred by a chain-gang of friends to an empty, undamaged shed. However, in the next few days many of these survivors of the hurricane succumbed, either through shock or the cold.

Mr and Mrs Lambert lost a total of 4,500 chickens, and although they struggled to maintain the business as best they could, loss of production due to the hurricane forced the closure of their poultry processing unit, making five of their staff redundant.

The cost to the Lamberts in financial terms was around £50,000.

Business continues today at Spring Elms Farm, but it's not quite Business As Usual.

Great ruts in the woodland floor. Smouldering debris and shredded leaning trees. This is the unhappy scene at Butcher's Wood, Danbury.

Photograph by Stephen Westover, Essex County Council

Nightmare in Chelmsford

CHELMSFORD Borough Council's radio system was put out of action when the aerial mast at Danbury was damaged by the storm, and a standby system was then set up in the council's emergency control room. The man at the sharp end of the hurricane emergency, Mr Kelvin Ward, said "All the council departments' resources were stretched to the limit."

As the winds wreaked havoc through mid-Essex the town's police station logged 1,010 calls between midnight on Thursday to 8.00 am on Friday. The Borough Council's Director of Housing, Mr Brian Platt, reported that his department had received more than 1,000 calls for help over the three days following the storm. Families from Stock, Galleywood and Boreham had to be rehoused when their mobile homes were wrecked by the winds, while both council employees and private contractors worked flat out to make stricken homes safe and weather-proof. To many elderly folk it was reminiscent of wartime.

There was mixed fortune for Mr Frank Smith and his wife who live in Great Baddow. The garage housing their Cortina was blown apart by the wind, but amazingly the car escaped with only minor damage. Also in Great Baddow a giant cedar collapsed onto a garage and some builders' huts, crushing them under its immense weight.

The Fire Brigade was kept busy answering an assortment of emergencies that ranged from dealing with dangerous chimneys, trees and flooding, to settling live power cables and freeing a horse that had become trapped in a Witham garage.

At the Carlton Riding School in Beehive Lane the roof of one of the stable blocks was lifted completely off, pulling one of the walls down.

Fortunately neither of the horses inside at the time was injured, but one was trapped in the wreckage and lost about four stone in weight.

Those London-bound commuters who braved the debris of the town found that the railway line was blocked and no trains were running, and the Eastern National bus company had to abandon its complete service on request from the police because of the danger of cross-winds and fallen trees.

All the town's parks lost trees, but the worst hit were Hylands Park and Oaklands Park where a 200 year-old specimen Turkey Oak was one of numerous victims. Just outside Chelmsford the Writtle Institute of Agriculture suffered losses of several fine trees, and a mobile greenhouse, which could be slid on runners to give protection to a number of crops, was destroyed by the winds.

Power supplies were interrupted to many homes in and around Chelmsford until late the following Monday as high voltage cables were torn down, causing extensive damage and forcing householders to im-provise their cooking and heating arrangements. Dennis Carlile, of Roxwell Road, managed to rig up emergency lighting with the aid of a car battery, an old headlamp and a radio. In the height of the storm Mr Carlile, his wife Cathy and daughter Carolyn braved the hurricane and went out to rescue their seven geese and 14 chickens. The geese were rehoused in the kitchen and the chickens in the lobby. Unfortunately the Carliles were unable to catch their ducks.

There was plain disappointment too, as well as fear and anguish, for the Princess Royal was due to make a visit to Broomfield Hospital on Black Friday to open a new ward block, but the helicopter that was to have been used to carry the royal visitor was unable to take off. Just before 9 o'clock the police were informed of the change of plan and were then able to release sorely-needed manpower onto storm-related work.

Residents at Temple Grove Caravan Park in West Hanningfield watched helplessly as the hurricane savaged their site. One of the caravans had its roof ripped away, and seven others were damaged by uprooted trees and flying branches. Considerable damage was also suffered by farmers in outlying areas when trees broke fences or gates, thus allowing livestock to stray onto busy roads. The directors of Chelmsford City Football Club were faced with the task of replacing part of the roof of The Barn and having the stadium's floodlights re-aligned after the winds had whipped them out of true.

Anglian Water found many rivers in their care to be blocked by fallen trees, giving rise to more fears of flooding. Engineers set out in teams to clear watercourses of their natural and unwelcome dams, especially along the Chelmer and the Cam.

To some Essex authorities October '87 must have appeared to be just one long nightmare.

Photograph by Claire Ogley

Staff of Broomfield Hospital hold the plaque that never was. The Princess, however, returned on November 27, 1987.

St. John Payne —topless

Photograph by Essex Chronicle Series

DURING the height of the hurricane Mr Colin Huggins, caretaker of the St John Payne School in Patching Hall Lane, Chelmsford, was so concerned for the security of the school that he went on a tour of inspection. Suddenly half the roof of a section of classrooms tore away. "It was terrifying," said Mr Huggins, "the winds must have been gusting at over 100 mph as they swept across the playing fields and blasted off half the roof."

The damage was horrific, and although contractors fitted a temporary roof and worked through the half-term to make the school safe, mobile classrooms had to be brought in to house some of the pupils.

The school is aided by the Catholic church authorities, and assistant director of education for the Brentwood Diocese, Mr David Squires, faced a daunting task, for not only had St John Payne lost its roof, he had other schools in his care with structural damage.

As for St John Payne, plans were drawn up, contractors approved and building work went on at the school through a good part of 1988, with pupils finally being returned to their re-roofed classrooms in January 1989. The cost of the work involved in restoring this school to its former weather-worthiness, was £361,700.

When the lights went out

HUGE skeleton-like pylons marching across the low Essex fields were damaged, and miles of overhead cables brought down either by the wind or by falling trees. Transformers were wrenched from the ground, poles snapped like twigs and the lights went out. Much of south-east England was plunged into darkness at the height of the storm, and many homes had no electricity for several days. In some remote villages and isolated farms it was a week or more before householders could dispense with Tilly lamps and makeshift meals cooked over an open fire.

A spokesman for the Eastern Electricity Board commented: "We had never experienced such devastation in the history of the EEB. It was an unprecedented situation." Approximately one in four of the Board's 2.8 million customers were affected, including 60 per cent of Anglian Water's installations. "We had a lot of dangerous situations with cables dangling and falling while still live," said Eastern Electricity's area manager David May.

Overnight the region faced a staggering amount of repairs, more than could normally be expected in a six-month period.

Fifteen helicopters were brought in to survey the lines and to locate faults. Tracked vehicles were used to transport heavy equipment, and EEB had to draft in 250 extra engineers and linesmen from places as far away as Northern Ireland, the Midlands, Yorkshire and Wales to join local crews in an all-out, round the clock effort to restore power to the beleagured county. This created its own nightmare of logistics, while materials also had to be rushed in to the area from suppliers in distant parts of the country.

The army sent men with special lifting gear to various corners of Essex to help clear one tangled mess after another, unravelling damaged transformers and cables from the mangled remnants of rain-soaked trees on clogged country lanes, and in some cases even installing temporary generators until normal power could be restored. The elderly residents of Orchard Lodge, Tiptree, had special reason to be grateful for the army's help when soldiers arrived with portable generators to bring light and heat to the 26 people at the home. "My residents think they're fantastic," said warden Cathy Austin.

Emergency generators were also delivered to convalescent homes, nursing homes and meat stores, while dairy farms in Frinton and Walton were thankful when portable generators were installed to help with milking.

Helplines were established at EEB offices giving advice on how to cope with the emergency, and with offers of food and warmth. Warnings were published too about the dangers associated with defrosted food as freezers began to thaw, and many hundreds of pounds' worth of food had to be disposed of in case of contamination.

Although 750,000 homes in East Anglia were initially thrown into darkness by the storm, within three days 675,000 customers had had their supplies restored, and by the fifth day there were just 40,000 remaining to be dealt with. But coming back on-power was not always universally welcomed, as some of the residents of North Weald will vouch when on the Sunday afternoon a sudden surge of too much electricity blew television sets and other electrical apparatus.

The hurricane inflicted the most costly and wide-spread damage of the Board's forty-year history. The east coast was the worst affected, but there was hardly one corner of the county that did not suffer an interruption of supplies.

When the engineers had at last brought light to East Anglia, many were then sent directly to Kent and Sussex to help their colleagues still battling against a continuing nightmare south of the Thames.

Eleven months later some of these same quiet heroes flew out to Jamaica to offer help to that devastated island in the wake of Hurricane Gilbert.

Photograph by Essex Chronicle Series

All over Essex electricity transformers were knocked down by falling trees. This one at Galleywood was dragged away, still attached to its pole. A new transformer was already in place.

An eye in the sky over Oaklands Park, Chelmsford shows some of the damage. A 200-year old Turkey Oak was among the victims.

47

Temporary repairs underway at Coldnailhurst Avenue, Braintree. On the roof of their parents home are David and Mark Robinson and friend Mike Coleman.

The windy city

THE experience of Colchester Borough Council in dealing with the hurricane crisis is probably typical of most authorities in Essex and East Anglia. It began in the dark early hours of Friday October 16 and went on throughout the day, but the effects of those winds on the town will be felt for many years after the event.

● At 3.50 am the council's emergency duty officer received a call from the Police who reported that Layer Road was blocked by fallen trees. Minutes later similar reports indicated other roads were blocked and the first of many sewage pumping stations was out of action.

● By 7 o'clock all key personnel and telephone operators who could get through had reported for duty. Normal work was suspended and additional telephones manned.

● By 8 o'clock further switchboards were opened. Incoming calls were arriving at the rate of one every three seconds during the first few hours of the emergency. More than 1,000 calls were handled that day.

● The housing division was almost deluged with calls from wardens, tenants and private householders pleading for help.

● Welcome offers of assistance with manpower, plant and chain saws came from individuals and contractors alike.

● Falling trees lifted large areas of pavement and roadway, and lorry loads of materials were rushed to several sites for emergency repairs to be carried out.

● Routine highway maintenance was abandoned, and it was not until the end of November that much of this work could be resumed.

● One conscientious road sweeper apologised that his work would not be up to his normal high standards, since he was experiencing difficulty with wind-blown debris!

● Damage to street lamps was extensive when the wind caused columns to whip in the same way as trees. Some snapped at ground level, others caused lamps to smash. Sixteen were found to be beyond repair and had to be completely replaced.

● The loss of electricity put 50 of the council's 70 sewage pumping stations out of action.

● 100 acres of woodland were devastated. In addition some 2,600 trees were lost from council administered land.

● As if the hurricane was not enough to contend with, at 10.00 am when the wind was abating, the Anglian Water Authority issued a flood warning and requested assistance from the Borough Engineer's Department.

● Some labour was diverted from emergency hurricane repair to fill 300 sandbags ready for distribution to properties most at risk.

Photograph by Terry Weeden, Essex Evening Gazette

A telephone kiosk and a postbox in Birch lie down in sympathy with the trees.

David Martin took this photograph of Clifton Lodge, London Road, Stanway, near Colchester buried beneath the limbs of a giant cedar of Lebanon. Imagine looking out of your bedroom window in the dark early hours and seeing a tree of this size falling onto your house?

50

Photograph by Adrian Rushton

Five adults smile and the baby gurgles with delight. This is British stoicism at its best for their house in Barrington Road, Colchester had collapsed around them. Pictured here (left to right) are baby Abbi, neighbour Kevin Clough, Traci Laurence, Nikki Long, Matthew Dutton and Julie Vaughan.

Roofless in Holland

MRS Day looks out of a roofless bedroom, exposed to the elements, with an expression that suggests the storm tried to hurt her family and neighbours, but failed. The roof of the Medusa Court flats in Holland was lifted off and deposited on the road outside blocking traffic for several hours. Ceilings crashed down on top of beds and forced residents to move to a downstairs flat where Norman and Vera Ludford supplied tea and coffee. Henry and Joan were sleeping when part of the roof fell on top of them. Mrs Day was hit on the head but not badly hurt. When she recovered from the intitial shock she looked up and saw storm clouds in place of her roof.

The devastated entertainment area at Tower Caravan Camp, Jaywick.

Photographs by Ken Clow

52

A familiar scene in Saffron Walden on the morning after when strenuous efforts were made to remove fallen trees. All roads in and out of the town were blocked and Saffron Walden police called in the army to help clear up the chaos. Teams of soldiers from the Royal Lancers at Carver Barracks arrived with chainsaws and stepped into the jungle to fight the good fight. Donald and Jane Benson, pictured here, did not need assistance from the army. They won their own battle!

Photograph by Saffron Walden Reporter

Nature makes amends for a night of fury

IN the aftermath of the hurricane there was an understandable sense of urgency to return life to normality as soon as possible. As distressing as it might have been for families to gaze at gaping holes in their roofs, or to haul trees from crushed cars and garages, most structural damage was put right before winter was out. In the majority of cases insurance claims were met with commendable speed and sympathy for the ordeal that so many had suffered.

Some major building works, naturally, took longer to carry out and in a few sad instances lives have been irrevocably changed by the effects of that unforgettable night. But what will take much longer to correct is the shape of our woodland landscapes; or rather, our concept of them.

To many of us the hurricane seemed at first like a disaster on a massive scale; a disaster almost too great to comprehend. The landscape had changed overnight, familiar views could no longer be recognised and it would take us a long time to come to terms with that fact. It is said that the south-east lost 40 per cent of its deciduous woods during the fifty years before the hurricane, and few people noticed. Yet suddenly, as we took stock of the situation immediately after the storm, millions of people were made aware of the importance of trees in the landscape, and that cannot be bad.

It was not a total disaster. Even in devastated woodlands all was not lost, and in terms of nature conservation few species will be adversely affected. The hurricane, it should be remembered, was an entirely natural phenomenon and it is clear that woodlands will regenerate themselves—with or without the help of man. Many plants, in fact, will directly benefit from newly created open spaces that now allow abundant light where before there was a crowding of shade, and countless birds and insects are attracted to dead and damaged timber. Where man is saddened by an 'untidy' sight, wildlife rejoices.

Most woods are not tidy parklands or neat gardens. They are wild, natural places and we need to come to terms with that fact—both as mere observers and as landowners with a management responsibility.

The Essex Naturalists' Trust cares for 71 nature reserves throughout the county, some forty of these having substantial woodland cover. In the path of the hurricane the Trust was faced with a monumental task of recovery, for in their 1,000 acres of ancient woodlands more than 20,000 mature trees had fallen. Copperas Wood near Tendring was probably the worst-hit woodland in all Essex with 25 acres razed to the ground. Blakes Wood at Danbury lost 4,000 trees and Weeley Hall Wood a thousand more.

But these are just the bare statistics of trees that were levelled. In addition there were many thousands of individuals left standing with severely damaged limbs, with crowns and branches torn off and all in need of tree surgery.

Even with considerable help from hundreds of volunteers in clearance operations, the financial cost to the Trust by June 1989 was more than £35,000, over £20,000 of which was raised by the Storm Appeal through donations from individuals, Trust Groups, Task Force Trees and the World Wide Fund for Nature.

Initially priorities had to be established and it was natural that the first thing to do was make the woodlands safe and take down dangerous trees. The Trust was conscious of the need to clear storm-felled timber without damaging habitats, in direct contrast to many private owners of woods who simply bulldozed their way through and caused more damage during clearance operations than was actually created by the wind. It was also important to save trees where possible, and the Trust made protests against felling where individuals could have been saved by tree surgery. Woodland Demonstration Days were held to explain how extraction could be sensitively managed with the use of horses, and how root-plates could be reseated to encourage toppled trees to regain their former upright stance.

In 1987 oak trees presented a bounty of acorns and many other species similarly produced an abundant harvest of seeds, so natural regeneration from fallen giants is expected to show dividends quite quickly. As these second-generation trees grow, so the age-range within the woodlands will be enriched.

Broadleaved woodlands offer Britain's richest habitat for insects, with more than 650 different types of beetle alone being found there. As for deadwood, this will steadily rot if allowed to lie, and as it does, so insects will proliferate; as insects increase, so birdlife benefits. The chain goes on and on.

Where some trees have had their crowns damaged, but not too severely to demand urgent surgery, exposed timber will entice woodpeckers and other woodland birds.

A number of wind-toppled trees have now been trimmed and reseated and are showing every sign of rejuvenation, as though through normal coppicing methods, while others that were felled by the storm but still had some root system intact, were left on the ground and are now throwing up a continuing growth. Chestnut in particular has responded with as much as two metres of growth in the two years since the hurricane. As they mature, malformed though some individuals may be, the woods will present a lively interest for future generations.

As for those huge discs of root-plates that still stand exposed, it has been found that wrens and even kingfishers have adopted them for nesting, and a number of the holes that were created when roots were wrenched out of the ground as the great trees fell have filled with water–to the benefit of newts and a variety of damp-loving plants.

Newly-created glades have allowed a revitalised flora, attracting butterflies where before no butterflies were to be seen. Anyone who has wandered through the countryside in the spring and early summer since that October day, will have noted with pleasure the increase in bluebells and foxgloves–direct gifts of the hurricane.

The hurricane blew a breath of fresh air through the countryside. Whilst it caused despair and heartache, and in some cases financial hardship, it has given landowners in retrospect a wonderful opportunity to take stock of their woodland practices. Mistakes that have been made in the past, in respect of single-species plantations dominating some areas and other trees being planted on unsuitable sites, can now be rectified.

We are all becoming more aware of the environment, more conscious of the vulnerable nature of the landscapes around us. The hurricane has given us breathing space, time to look at exactly what it is we require of our fast disappearing countryside, and of our place in it.

Many local authorities have replanted street-side trees where they lost specimens to the storm. Parks have been restocked and in some cases landscaped. Would it not be comforting to discover too that farmers and landowners throughout Essex and East Anglia have been fired with enthusiasm and determination to put right the enormous losses that have occurred to our broadleaved woodlands in the fifty years before the hurricane?

The impact of the hurricane of October 16 1987 will be visible on the woodland landscape of Essex for a number of years to come. The widespread loss of mature trees will take decades to replace. Yet new life is already springing out of the acres of destruction and the future is one of hope and expectation.

Nature is doing her best to make amends for a night of fury. Are we sensitive enough to do our bit too?

Photograph by G. R. Mortimer

ONE of the victims of the Great Storm in Mistley was a splendid horse chestnut tree planted 85 years earlier to commemorate the coronation of King Edward VII in 1902. The tree, which stood on a triangle of land opposite the well-known Adam Towers (the twin remains of a long-demolished church), had given summer shade to generations of Mistley's villagers who rested on the seats that surrounded it.

When the tree fell across the road it also broke the column off the village war memorial. An appeal was launched for its replacement, and more than £1,300 was raised among local residents and companies within weeks. "They have done extremely well for us," said Mr Ivan Garwood, the appeal organiser.

The stump of the original horse chestnut was removed and a mature replacement planted in its place that winter. There was also sufficient money in the appeal to repair the seat and generally improve the site, while the repair to the war memorial was met by the Council's insurance company.

Cambridge Grief

CAMBRIDGESHIRE with its predominance of open prairie-like farmland and fens is no stranger to the destruction that can be wrought by freak winds. Furious gales occurred in January 1974 and hurricane-force winds exactly two years later in January 1976, both causing widespread disruption.

A remarkable tornado was experienced in May 1950 which ran a 65-mile path from Wendover in Buckinghamshire passing over Woburn Park, Lidlington, Earith, Covenay, Witcham and Sutton—spawning an offshoot to Kimbolton.

The morning of October 16, 1987 provided Cambridge weatherman Peter Ashton with two records. The fiercest wind, at 100 mph, he had recorded at Cambridge in 54 years of amateur meteorology, and the lowest barometric reading.

The damage to trees was great. Three hundred were lost in the city and several people in the area recorded lucky escapes when their houses in Duxford were hit. The most unusual must have been the escape of two lorry drivers who were having an early breakfast at 4 am when the chimney of the next-door accommodation fell through the roof on-to the table next to them at the Autostop Cafe, New Wimpole.

Animals fared badly; a complete aviary belonging to Donald and Marilyn Ward was tossed over a bush and into the neighbouring field with the loss of 30 birds. A sheep and a cow were killed at Wimpole Hall where several trees fell including a 300 year-old lime.

In the following days when 2,000 homes were without electricity, horses at Kings Ride stables near Royston in Herts lost their water supply and local firemen came to the rescue bringing water by the bucketfull twice a day.

East Anglian firemen were also involved in a nervewracking ordeal near Wisbech when their fire engine turned a corner on the Low Common road to Tydd St Mary to be confronted by a huge willow falling across their path. They reversed hurriedly as more trees in the line began to topple.

Anglesey Abbey features sculptures against a backdrop of ancient trees and is renowned for the peacefulness which pervades the air. This was rudely shattered when many valuable trees fell creating chaos for the gardeners that morning. The greatest drama, however, occurred at the Wandlebury Estate, south east of Cambridge in the Gog Magog Hills.

As Bill Clark the warden went to bed on the night of October 15 he heard that 40 mph winds were forecast and prepared for a possible loss of electricity as trees fell. Waking briefly in the night he was aware of the ferocity of the wind but was still totally unprepared for what he was to behold the following morning.

"When we woke up we thought there was a fire; our room was ablaze with light, where normally we never saw the sun in our bedroom because of the height of the surrounding trees."

The windows at the front of the house were besmirched with leaves hurled against the glass and Bill was moved to tears to see the chaos and the loss of so many majestic old friends. The enormity of the task before him filled him with dread.

When asked to go on radio and television it was the last thing he felt like doing; he wanted to crawl away and hide in some dark place.

However, he responded to the request of the media and gave such a moving and passionate account of what had happened at Wandlebury that cheques started pouring in from wellwishers to help with the clearing up and replanting. More than 1,000 trees fell at Wandlebury and such was the feeling of grief in the city that the Tree Appeal launched by Cambridge Preservation Society and supported by the Cambridge Evening News reached £7,000 by November 1987.

The fund continued to grow in the New Year. The County Council contributed £14,000 and £7,000 came from Task Force Trees. By February Bill Clark had planted 2,700 trees and his wife, Wendy, grew saplings from seeds saved from the largest beeches.

The following year she traced the great great great great granddaughter of Peter Tapfield, the founder of Wandlebury Woods, and she came from Canada to plant the new saplings.

Bill Clark, senior warden at Wandlebury with one of the young trees which he has nursed through the drought.

Photograph by Cambridge Evening News

Racing history of an unusual kind was made at Newmarket on October 16, 1987 when a meeting was abandoned for the first time since 1908. There were chaotic scenes at the racecourse followed by a frantic but effective clearing up operation which enabled The Cesarewitch the following day to go ahead as planned. However, racegoers heading for the Rowley Mile course faced several diversions due to fallen trees.

Thomas Barber of Alconbury west of Cambridge was three in October 1987, when the big storm was followed by very heavy rainfall, leaving him with a very big puddle to play in.

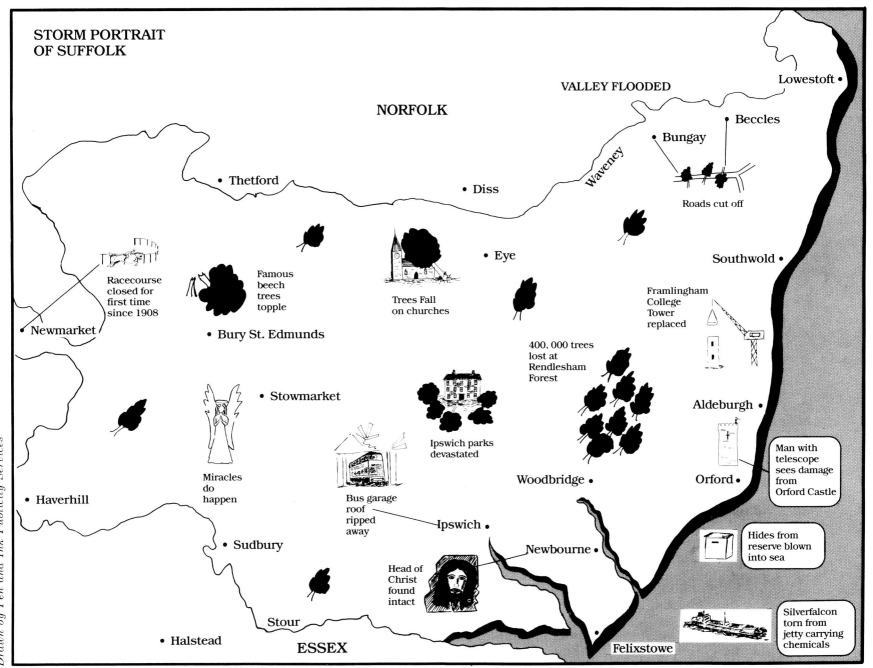

STORM PORTRAIT
OF SUFFOLK

NORFOLK

VALLEY FLOODED

Lowestoft •

• Beccles

• Bungay

Waveney

Roads cut off

• Thetford

• Diss

• Eye

Southwold •

Racecourse
closed for
first time
since 1908

Famous
beech
trees
topple

Trees Fall
on churches

Framlingham
College
Tower
replaced

• Newmarket

• Bury St. Edmunds

400, 000 trees
lost at
Rendlesham
Forest

Aldeburgh •

• Stowmarket

Ipswich parks
devastated

Miracles
do
happen

Woodbridge •

Orford •

Man with
telescope
sees damage
from
Orford Castle

• Haverhill

Bus garage
roof
ripped
away

Ipswich •

Newbourne •

Hides from
reserve blown
into sea

• Sudbury

Head of
Christ
found
intact

Stour

Felixstowe

Silverfalcon
torn from
jetty carrying
chemicals

• Halstead

ESSEX

Drawn by Pen and Ink Publicity Services

59

God's houses suffer in Suffolk

SOME people in North Essex believe they live in East Anglia. That is not so. The essential East Anglian is an inhabitant of Norfolk and Suffolk (north folk and south folk). They have Viking blood in their veins and they like to think of East Anglia as an island—the like of which exists nowhere else in England. This is enhanced geographically by the pugnacious way in which East Anglia juts its great strong jaw into the North Sea.

Suffolkers in particular see themselves as very much a race apart from the rest of England. It is the most eastern county and one of the largest with an area of 1,481 square miles. There are wide heaths as purple as the moors of Scotland, 40,000 acres of forestry plantations, a tapestry of great woods, marshland, coastal villages which have kept their souls and magnificent churches.

This is where the Great Storm was particularly cruel for it developed a penchant for attacking Suffolk's churches and in this respect showed a curious lack of denominational discrimination. It demolished Cransford Baptist Church, blew an east wall out of the parish church of Newbourne and felled the Methodist Church of Trimley. Roofs were ripped off a Catholic chapel in Leiston, three trees fell onto the parish church of Thelnetham and one giant cedar onto Westhall near Halesworth. Ditchingham lost a pinnacle on top of its tower, St. Edmund's at Southwold a flagstaff and weathervane and St. Mary's Church, Uggeshall, not wanting to be outdone by Newbourne, lost an east wall including a stained glass window depicting the Crucifixion.

The wind played tricks with transport in Suffolk. No matter how strong the vehicle the wind was stronger. Huge aluminium girders were ripped off the Ipswich bus garage and wrapped around a row of double deckers, an articulated lorry was blown over on the Orwell Bridge, aeroplanes were upturned and boats on the Broads were ripped from their moorings and drifted helplessly down swollen rivers.

Suffolk is a flat county, the highest point being at Rede which reaches only some 420 feet above sea level. Despite all that has been said about the devastation on the downs and ridges of Kent and Sussex, Suffolk suffered as much as anywhere. If sturdy buildings of some stature were vulnerable then the aged Scots and Corsican pines in the Rendlesham, Tunstall and Dunwich forests stood no chance. The wind snapped or unrooted trees in their thousands. The Forestry Commission estimated that up to 80 per cent of the forest fell and immediately after the storm people drove to Rendlesham just to stare at the shredded and splintered forest. It was an awesome sight.

Although more trees were lost in Suffolk than in the more talked-about county of Kent, luckily there were no fatalities but miracles galore. Tracy Sharman of Ipswich had just left her bedroom when a tree crashed through the roof and onto the bed. Baby Megan McSloy lay asleep just 15 yards from the resting place of a Turkey Oak. June Laplace of Ipswich was trapped under a pile of bricks. She was rescued by her son. John Paul of Bramford Road was in his bedroom when the ceiling collapsed and Basil and Henrietta Gladden were actually in bed when a chimney fell on their bedroom. They all escaped injury.

There were some lucky motorists. Co-op milkman Keith Joy of Chantry found the road blocked ahead of him. He went for help and on his return found the vehicle was a mangled wreck. There was a similar story for Andrew Brame of Ipswich and a woman from Syleham was actually hit by a falling tree at Hoxne and taken to hospital. At Nowton two cows were crushed to death.

The damage to urban trees was as great as that in the countryside where every road in the north of Suffolk was blocked and every village cut off from its neighbour. The East Anglian rail network was also paralysed and only the Norwich to Lowestoft service managed to operate.

By 8 am on this memorable morning the wind had dropped below gale force across southern and eastern England except for the coastal areas of Suffolk and Norfolk. Here there was heavy rain which just added to the problem because most of Suffolk was already on flood alert.

Schools throughout the county closed but not before parents had criticised education chiefs for their indecision. In fact Radio Orwell made an on-the-air appeal for a senior member of the education department to contact them to clear up the confusion.

In adversity the people of Suffolk were drawn together and the photographs on the following pages show, not only the results of the morning's mayhem but the willingness to bring comfort to neighbours in distress. Gordon Blyth of Beccles knows what this means. When tiles blew from his roof he collected them up and stacked them next to a fuel tank. They were stolen—at least that is what Gordon thought. The street lights came on a few days later illuminating his roof and there instead of gaping holes were Gordon's tiles. The Good Samaritans were two jolly neighbours.

Dignity returns to Ipswich

EXPERTS estimate that it took just 80 minutes to destroy the dignity of the Ipswich parks. In those few furious moments the picturesque, carefully nurtured landscape was transformed to a tangled wreckage. Carcasses of once-proud oaks littered the ground, ancient cedars, tall, handsome pines, leafy limes and monkey puzzles were all casualties, limbs smashed and roots exposed.

The legacy of this terrible night stunned the people of Ipswich, for the damage was found to be more widespread than originally thought. With hundreds of broken branches hanging precariously over pathways and favourite walks the council banned the public from entering the parks. The clearing-up operation alone, they said, would take many months.

With careful surgery and dedication, a helping hand from nature and with the support of a caring community, the tranquillity of the parks began to return, albeit slowly. Those who were so heartbroken in October 1987 often look at the landscape today and marvel at the reformation.

Although, as yet, there is no comparison with the former beauty, the council's parks manager, Simon Cook, the director of recreation and amenities, Joe Orr and the man co-ordinating the restoration work, Martin Minta or "Mr Trees" as he is called, performed miracles in a joint operation with nature and, of course, time. The work will not be completed for many years.

The storm placed a high premium on the skill of the arborists who carefully pruned the trees which survived. Roped, almost lovingly, to the trees the surgeons worked long hours to remove dangerous branches and produce a pleasing shape. Saplings were planted with care for not all trees are suitable for town parks. Rowan, Holly, Hazel, Field Maple and Yew were considered to be suitable species and aesthetically pleasing.

Today the Park chiefs and their team of contractors often consider the mammoth problem which they helped to overcome. It was a problem on a scale beyond anyone's experience and began with the formation of a group consisting of borough councillors, officers and conservation experts.

The councillor leading the group, Mrs Sheila Baguley said at the time. "The hurricane struck our hearts. It will be good to have something to channel our anger into."

There is no longer anger in the hearts, anger in the letters to newspapers or anger in the parks in the shape of twisted limbs. The people of Ipswich understood the enormity of the task and appreciated the skill and enthusiasm which marked the start of an amazing recovery.

Photograph by Ipswich Borough Council

Work at height with cutting tools called for concentration and a high degree of skill.

Photograph by N. J. Cotterell

Photograph by Holly Pelling

Nothing is forever, not even trees. This is Chantry Park, Ipswich before and after the storm. The tranquillity is still there but a mighty friend is missing.

Last respects to the fallen

Photograph by East Anglian Daily Times

PROTECTED against heavy rain and framed by the jaws of a mutilated tree, which seems about to gobble them up, this small group of Ipswich people appear to be rooted to the spot and unable to escape from their impending fate.

This was the forlorn scene in Christchurch Park, Ipswich early in 1988 when the Borough's parks department organised a guided tour for those who wished to pay their last respects to the fallen—187 trees in Christchurch and more than 1,000 in all the town's parks.

Such was the damage in Ipswich's parks, aboretums, recreation grounds and cemeteries that it had been necessary to close them all for safety reasons. The group of people pictured here were among the first to see the extent of the wreckage.

In the weeks to come more guided tours were arranged in Ipswich and an exhibition mounted to demonstrate the danger which existed in the parks. This included pictures to illustrate the effect on wildlife, project work completed by children and a display of turned wood, abstract shapes and carvings. Thousands visited the Cornhill and helped to swell the Ipswich Tree Appeal.

A visit to any one of the parks today will provide tangible evidence that the appeal money was well spent.

Photograph by East Anglian Daily Times

There was not much left of the patients' social centre at St. Clements Hospital, Ipswich. Mr Jack Bull, voluntary services co-ordinator points to the two walls blown-in by the force of the wind. The centre provided an important recreational facility for patients at the psychiatric hospital and after the storm they had to make do with the hospital church for their activities. "It was far from ideal" said Mr Bull, "in view of the lack of facilities such as no toilets". This situation lasted for 18 months during which time Suffolk Health Authority approved the funding for rebuilding, at a cost of £23,000. "It was 18 months of real trauma" said Mr Bull. During this period VOSDA (Voluntary Services Development Association) organised a series of fund raising events and, with the support of the local paper and a terrific response from the people of Ipswich raised £10,000 which paid for the refurbishing of the centre. They were able to move back in March 1989 and the official opening took place on August 18.

This was the sight which greeted bus drivers when they arrived at the Constantine Road depot in Ipswich on the morning of the storm. Giant strips of aluminium cladding were wrapped around a row of double decks, putting them and the depot out of action.

Tim Gray (second left) of Felix Arc Marine with his team Jonathan Luke (seated), John Gray, Gary Kingston and Pat Ryan. They boarded the Silverfalcon as she listed badly with a 'time bomb' aboard.

The most expensive night ever

SOON after the storm the Government issued guidelines on compensation and suggested that insurance companies might be too ponderous in dealing with claims. Newspapers speculated on the magnitude of the catastrophe and wondered how the insurance industry could bring peace of mind to a hundred thousand disturbed and shattered lives.

In fact all major insurers were quickly into top gear and responded with a resolve that has done much to enhance the reputation of the insurance market. Millions of calls poured into overworked claims offices with policy holders requesting advice on a variety of incidents. When the roads were re-opened, telephone and electricity supplies restored and a degree of normality returned, the insurance companies remained alone to absorb the implications of the most expensive night Britain has ever known.

As the staff of the Norwich Union's head office picked their way round fallen trees to get to work that morning they knew one thing for certain: there were going to be a lot of claims. Drastic action had to be taken.

Like all major insurers Norwich Union set up an emergency claims unit dedicated solely to hurricane claims, so its normal service would not be disrupted. Advertisements were placed in newspapers; and local radio gave special emergency telephone numbers. Volunteer staff from branches unaffected by the storm, came to the aid of their head office colleagues. At its peak there were 45 people in the Norwich Union unit.

At first policyholders were asking advice on what work they could put in hand before sending a claim. Then, gathering momentum, the claims rolled in with no less than 1,500 being notified on one day. During this period the staff were working a 12-hour day, six days a week.

Claims on Norwich Union householders' policies rose to more than 43,000 involving payments of over £25 million. There were, of course, many more hurricane-related claims for commercial buildings and motor vehicles. When these were added the figure rose to around £45 million for more than 50,000 claims.

Perhaps the most surprising aspect was that long after the Emergency Unit had been run down, claims were still arriving in a steady trickle. This is because some policyholders, especially in the worst affected areas, had found it difficult to get hold of builders and materials in order to get repair work completed. Eighteen months after the storm one or two of these accounts were still coming in.

'Time bomb' at Felixstowe

THE 1,300 ton British tanker, Silverfalcon was securely moored alongside the oil jetty at Felixstowe port when the hurricane blew in. She was loaded with industrial chemicals and the crew on board, which included 13 officers, became more and more concerned as the winds increased in intensity. The men knew they were sitting on a potential 'time bomb'.

The harbour waters began to heave and fall, storm-whipped waves crashed against the side of the tanker and spray was blown through the funnel into the engine room. A massive gust tore the ship away from the jetty, ripping off the wooden fencing and damaging the jetty itself. Concern now gave way to a full alert. If the toxic gases should explode that would be the end of the Silverfalcon. Such fears fuelled a massive emergency operation.

Men and women going to work at Felixstowe Port were turned away, the area was sealed off and hundreds of people nearby evacuated from their homes. The tug Ganges drew alongside and a rope was thrown to second officer, Michael Nicholson. Hardly able to stand in the teeth of the gale, he slipped and fell but grabbed a rail and narrowly escaped being washed overboard.

By now the wind was hurling the tanker against the side of the jetty. She had lost the propellor and all around drifting or sinking barges were being torpedoed into the jetty. Sparks were flying and the crew could almost hear the 'time bomb' ticking.

Heroes of the hour were Tim Gray, a salvage expert and his colleagues Pat Ryan, Gary Kingston, Jonathan Luke and John Gray. They boarded the Silverfalcon as the bruised and battered crew scrambled to safety. By now the vessel was listing and appeared to be on the verge of breaking up. She was holed in three places above the water line but mercifully the inner skin of the double hull near the cargo tank was not punctured.

As the winds subsided the most menacing chemical, propanol, was made safe with a nitrogen 'blanket' and ethylene diamine was discharged. Felixstowe oil jetty was too badly damaged to allow the unloading of the remaining chemicals and so Gray and his men towed the damaged tanker to Ipswich Dock where eventually she was repaired.

Felixstowe Port was reopened at 4 pm on Friday afternoon, about eight hours after the drama began.

The damaged Silverfalcon—safely back at Ipswich.

Photographs by East Anglian Daily Times

She was badly holed.

The Earl William—she broke free from her moorings.

Ordeal at Sea

THE Tamil detainees who managed to slip out of Sri Lanka and seek entry in Britain as refugees from their war-torn island had every justification in believing that the danger back home was preferable to their harrowing ordeal in England on October 16, 1987.

Earl William, a Sealink ferry, had been chartered by the Home Office to serve as a detention ship for immigrants who were waiting for their claims to enter Britain to be heard. Among them were the Tamils who had converted savings into airline tickets and were looking anxiously for refugee status.

For five uncomfortable months they were confined to the old ferry and to ensure there was no escape a roll call was taken each night and the detainees locked in their cabins. Conditions were bad according to the Seaman's Union. Newspapers compared the Earl William with the old-time prison hulks.

The ship was moored near Harwich on the Essex side of the Stour but in the early hours of that night with the wind at its zenith the old vessel broke free and rolled into the estuary with nobody in control.

The detainees were scared stiff as the ship lurched away from St. George's Quay and smashed into anchored yachts, sinking several. She drifted 200-300 yards hitting a small barge moored nearby. This holed the hull of the Earl William near an engine room storeroom. Water came in but the gash was above the waterline.

The Earl William dropped both anchors but they didn't hold. Three tugs tried unsuccessfully to hold her—but to no avail. At that point a daring helicopter rescue was considered by the Harbour Board but this was abandoned as the tide slipped out and the ship came to rest on sand at Shotley Point.

The Tamils were in a terrible state but all ended happily. The detainees were taken off the Earl William and the Home Office agreed to give them temporary admission to live with relatives or sponsors. A coach took them to the Tamil Temple at Wimbledon.

By now they were jubilant. They were free to live in the community thanks to the Home Office and, more important, to the hand of nature.

Forester Phil Scott at the Cliff Plantation.

Photograph by Ipswich Evening Star

Pin Mill—a vision of the future

THE Cliff Plantation at Pin Mill on the south bank of the River Orwell was a 42-acre conifer planation bought by the National Trust to use as a crop to subsidise its conservation work in the region. The storm changed the landscape overnight. In place of a forest on a quiet corner of the Suffolk coastline there were thouands of uprooted trees and large gaping holes in the woodland. Pin Mill was considered to have suffered the greatest percentage loss of trees in the National Trust's East Anglia region.

The scars of that night are fading fast and the next generation will easily miss the marks of this instant landscape evolution. Pin Mill has undergone a transformation, almost like an ageing process in reverse.

In place of mature pines, tiny saplings, 43,000 of them are sprouting into trees. The National Trust have replanted Corsican pine as a cash crop but there is also oak, beech, chestnut and cherry. The lopsided stumps have gone and colonies of willowherb and blackberries keep company with the saplings. There is more light, more air and panoramic views across the Orwell.

Many people have been involved with the Pin Mill story but two names are prominent. One is forester, Phil Scott whose restoration plan was carried out with a quiet determination. Following forestry guidelines, he has created an environment which will only be seen at its best by the next generation.

The other is Mrs Carol Carver who lives at Martlesham Heath, Ipswich. On the death of her husband William, who loved the Suffolk countryside, she invited friends to contribute towards the cost of trees rather than pay for a memorial service. The result is several hundred hardwood trees, planted in a large clump marking a footpath and a stand overlooking the Orwell. The skyline will be English—oak, ash, beech and chestnut.

Pin Mill Wood today is a true vision of the future. **See page 82**

Photographs by Debbie Wolmarans

Memorial to a storm

THE chapel tower at Framlingham College, a landmark for many miles around, was substantially built as a memorial to Queen Victoria's husband Albert in the early nineteenth century but like the trees in the college grounds it was unable to withstand the vicious buffeting. When the storm subsided horrified onlookers saw the tower was split in two and the spire was precariously bridging the gap.

Headmaster, Mr Laurie Rimmer, feared the tower would topple on to his house but eventually decided he was reasonably safe. A crack, 18 inches wide, ran up the tower and the spire was hanging at an angle. Another gust would have brought masonry and timber crashing down so the area below was immediately declared out of bounds.

School officials quickly decided that the whole structure should be replaced and within a few weeks the tower was repaired and a new spire added. This remains as a memorial, not to a Prince, but to an historic storm.

These two dramatic pictures of the spire being removed tell their own story. They were taken by Miss Debbie Wolmarans who works at Framlingham College.

Photograph by: Steve Scott, Forestry Commission

The tree nursery in the polytunnels at Rendlesham after the storm.

The fallen forest

ON a warm October day in 1987, some time after the Great Storm, a lone traveller arrived at Rendlesham to see for himself if stories he had heard about this violent wind were really true. He stepped out of his car near Claypond and, in growing disbelief just stared at the decapitated forest. Hundreds of thousands of Scots and Corsican pines were snapped off below the half way mark, entire root systems were lifted out of the ground. There was an eerie silence; the birds had gone and there was calm, a funereal calm soon to be replaced by the song of the chainsaw and the thump of the axe.

It was almost as if this rampaging wind had a particular grievance against the Forestry Commission on its journey through Suffolk. The damage wreaked to Rendlesham, Tunstall and Dunwich was considered to be on a scale greater than any other part of southern England.

An aerial survey was organised, a stereoscopic set of photographs closely studied and a computer forecast provided these amazing statistics—400,000 trees lost at Rendlesham, 300,000 at Tunstall and 260,000 at Dunwich. Put another way there were 13 years wood supply in various horizontal angles and it had to be extracted.

Warden Bob Hands and his indomitable team realised that no-one had experienced a problem of this magnitude. The gale of 1976 caused immense damage but the losses then were a mere fraction compared to the 475,000 cubic metres of wood now lying on the ground.

Mr Hands may have felt a personal loss but he was quickly to the forefront of the battle to remove the fallen timber. He was joined by 15 men employed by the district office at Woodbridge and a further 50 men with all their machinery. Forestry Commission specialists retrained the men and a safe, economical and practical method of clearance quickly got underway.

Almost all the wood was cut manually with chainsaws and removed by large purpose-built forwarders fitted with hydraulic cranes for loading and unloading. The rough terrain was suddenly a hive of activity. Skidders, harvesters, grinders, shredders, stump gobblers and a massive convoy of lorries were employed. By mid summer 1989, 350,000 cubic metres of wood had been cleared. If you consider that a wagon can carry around 20 cubic metres this volume equates to 17,500 lorries loaded—and there was a long way to go!

Once the ground was cleared of wood a contractor chipped the branches, waste and tops to make garden mulch. Stumps were gouged out and the skeletons heaped into long lines across the compartment—reminiscent almost of first world war gravestones. There was no burning in Rendlesham, Tunstall or Dunwich as this was a huge risk to the uncleared areas.

Just like a battlefield. Rendlesham Forest after the storm.

Photograph by Simon Hodges

For months this activity has continued in the fallen forests and the Forestry Commission expect to complete the job by April 1990. Replanting has also been undertaken by mechanical means using Corsican pine seedlings grown individually in paper tubes. About 2,500 trees per hectare are planted which is followed by a weeding regime involving mechanical and chemical control.

What is happening to the extracted timber? Paul Johnston, district forester responsible for marketing said that 75,000 cubic metres of wood is being stored under water sprinklers at Lynford, near Thetford. This will be sold over a few years. The rest of the wood is going to sawmills who buy it at the twice-yearly auctions. A lot has gone to Sweden to be made into paper pulp.

As the forest crusaders continue their relentless battle with the prostrate pines that lone traveller, and many like him, are still trying to absorb the loss of the trees. Rendlesham was the last stronghold for the red squirrel and 80 per cent of the trees they inhabited were destroyed. Bats, a nationally protected species, also had a hard time and 200 bat boxes were lost. Robins, blue tits, wrens, blackbirds, great tits have gone, but in time they will all come back.

It took 60 years for the saplings, planted in the early '20's, to grow into a great tall forest. On the morning of October 16, 1987 hurricane winds took 80 minutes to destroy it.

Life for the long-distance lorry driver, it is said, is a lonely one. It is even more lonely when you're upside down on the great expanse of the Orwell Bridge with not another vehicle in sight and the wind is blowing at 70 mph. This photograph of a lorry en route to the Brain Haulage depot in Ipswich was taken early on the Friday morning when the headlights were still ablaze. The strength of the wind across the Orwell was awesome. The picture, in fact, tells its own story.

No place to hide

JOHN PARTRIDGE, warden of the RSPB Reserve at Havergate Island, climbed to the top of Orford Castle with his telescope to check on the state of the reserve on the morning of the storm. What he saw was the sad sight of two collapsed hides on the island and two more floating on the North Sea.

From his vantage point John also saw how the wind had played games with the small boats and crafts wherever they were moored. Many were washed ashore, others had capsized in the sea. The motor boat *Gwel Marten* was crushed between the quay and a larger vessel.

The loss of the *Gwel Marten* was part of a double tragedy for the warden. The Gwel Marten was the RSPB boat for passengers from Orford to Havergate Island and she was badly damaged. An appeal was launched, so successfully that funds were sufficient to buy a purpose-built boat and repair some of the damaged hides.

'I was lucky', said John, 'in having a RSPB group at Woodbridge. Members helped me to strip down most of the damaged hides and rebuild with the original timber. One was totally destroyed so we had to make a new one.'

In retrospect the wind blew some good in the direction of both Orford and Havergate Island. More visitors and sturdy new hides are two of the benefits. The avocets are breeding again and there is a smart modern boat to carry the passengers. Its name, appropriately, is *October Storm*.

Photograph by John Gardiner

A *picture that says quite a lot. A boat that has drifted onto a country road, a yellow BT van, a flooded lane and trees in full leaf. This was a more peaceful Suffolk scene near Chillesford on October 16, 1987.*

Photograph by Fern Flynn

A second blow

This strip of storm-ravaged land lies between the Ipswich to Felixstowe railway and the old A45, close to the village of Nacton. It is part of the Orwell Park Estate which lost more than 150 acres of woodland of which 75 per cent were hardwood trees. The storm came up the Orwell estuary and showed no mercy for the trees on either bank. Pinmill on the southern side had similar damage but at Orwell Park it attacked the central cone of trees, a characteristic repeated in places across southern England. This aerial picture was supplied by Martin Freeman of Strutt and Parker in Ipswich. Mr Freeman is the agent for the privately owned Orwell park and is to the forefront in an exciting restoration project.

THE depression which moved across Scotland into the North Sea on January 2, 1976 and deepened dramatically over the Norfolk coastline produced hurricane force winds that rampaged violently across the countryside. We will never experience a gale of such ferocity again, East Anglians said at the time.

Lord and Lady Somerleyton's 720-acre estate in north-east Suffolk, close to the sea, caught the full fury of that night and lost thousands of trees. Clearing up and careful replanting followed and by 1987 the gardens of Somerleyton Hall and the landscaped Country Park of Fritton were looking better than ever.

Then came the second storm.

This time rare and ancient trees in the garden were lost and dozens of oaks and beeches fell in the park. 'The disastrous weather has undone all our work and created more,' Lord Somerleyton said at the time. It was an understatement. 250 trees were down in one plantation alone. The village of Somerleyton was cut off. There was no electricity and villagers cooked on open fires.

His Lordship's never-say-die attitude and the devotion of those around him has helped the estate towards a second recovery. Tranquillity has returned to Somerleyton but there is still much to be done.

See page 88

Miracles do happen

DO you believe in miracles? The McSloy family of Melford Road, Stowmarket do ... and so do the Foulger's from the same road, and the Sharman's, the Gladden's, the Paul's and the Laplace's from Ipswich. In fact there are scores of families who missed death or serious injury by a whisker—and that was in a county where an estimated 750,000 trees fell. A miracle indeed.

Megan McSloy was just 10 months old in October 1987 and was asleep in her bedroom when an enormous Turkey Oak landed less than 15 feet from where she lay. It demolished a garage and the porch roofs of three houses were badly damaged. Neighbour Mrs Suzanne Foulger heard a knocking against the window and actually looked out in time to see the tree coming towards her. She didn't hang around to see the result.

The two families and those next door were evacuated by firemen and because of the threat from another large oak tree in a neighbouring back garden the McSloy's never returned.

Tracy Sharman of Milden Road, Ipswich, who was 19 at the time, was even luckier. A tree actually came through the roof of her bedroom and landed on the bed just two minutes after she had left the room. Tracy who was woken by the wind, was petrified and tried to hide under the covers. Eventually she decided to go into her mother's bedroom where she heard 'an almighty crash'. Her bedroom was full of debris and branches.

Donald and June Laplace of Rendelsham Road, Ipswich possibly owe their lives to their son, Sinclair. During the night the roof of their house fell in and bricks, tiles and plasterboard fell onto their bed. Sinclair ran to their room, opened the door and found choking dust and rubble. His mother was trapped under a pile of bricks but he managed to pull her out of the bed. As they were about to go downstairs the rest of the ceiling and roof fell in.

Basil and Henrietta Gladden are thankful that they made the decision to re-roof their house in Wherstead Road, Ipswich just before the storm. The pensioners had a rude awakening when the chimney stack collapsed and came to rest in the rafters above their bed. They were certain the old roof would have given way under the weight of the fallen chimney.

John Paul of Bramford Road, Ipswich was woken by the wind and heard tiles being whipped off the roof by the wind. He took his wife and family downstairs where they sat for about two hours listening to the storm. At 7 am he went upstairs again and was in his bedroom when part of the gable wall of the house was blown in, followed by the ceiling collapsing just inches from where he was standing.

Photographs by Fern Flynn

This is the threatening Oak tree which prompted the McSloy family to move from their badly-damaged house in Melford Road, Ipswich—never to return. Inset shows Megan and her sister in the doorway of their new home.

Photograph by Fern Flynn

Tracy Sharman of Milden Road, Ipswich points to her bedroom where a tree came through the roof and landed on her bed, just two minutes after she had left the room.

Photograph by East Anglian Daily Times

In a scene more reminiscent of the aftermath of the blitz a resident of Stowmarket contemplates the enormous task ahead of him. Bob Foulger's house in Melford Road was hit by a falling tree which also damaged two other houses and completely demolished a garage. Like other towns in Suffolk, Stowmarket was cut off but it was water, not wind, which made the Ipswich Road a no-go area. Here the River Rat lived up to its name and flooded the main route into the town. Firemen faced with numerous other tasks decided not to pump the notorious flood zone in the basin of the Rat but leave it to drain naturally. In other areas the River Gipping also rose to danger level and Mid-Suffolk handed out hundreds of sandbags to residents of Regents Street and Cardinals Road. An all-night vigil was mounted but the sandbags saved the day.

Ben Platts-Mills and his colleagues won a special prize in an environmental competition for 'the exciting and artistic way in which they have communicated with nature.' Ben is pictured here (second left) with some of the judges in the early stages of the project.

Eye and the storm

BEN Platts-Mills, who lives close to the ancient market town of Eye where he is chairman of the community council and an ardent conservationist, had every reason to feel personally bereaved by the events of October 16, 1987.

The Town Moor Woods which he was helping to restore from a jungle of neglect looked like a Paul Nash painting of The Somme. Whole trees were snapped off between 12 and 15 feet from the ground. Many were suspended and fractured and hundreds lay in a tangled heap.

Ben, a landscape artist, put down his paintbrushes and picked up a pen to write a programme of work and an axe to clear the woods. He saw in the 28 acres of Town Moor, not a tragedy but, an opportunity to create a monument to that night.

The storm had given him the opportunity to develop the area into an expanded environment for wildlife and wildlife watchers alike. He thought carefully about the task ahead and how he could use his artistic skills to create the storm memorial. Ben sought professional advice on making the woods safe and training the volunteers that would be needed in the years to come. He looked for publicity and funds. With support from the people of Eye the artist set to work on his largest canvas yet—one which measured more than 14 acres.

Town Moor, once rough meadowland and scrub, site of the town's refuse dump and a plantation of diseased willows, has undergone a transformation that is more aesthetically pleasing, more dramatic and more adventurous than even Ben Platts-Mills ever intended.

Around the stumps of those shattered poplars he has created a maze which twists and turns in an intricate pattern of pathways. A viewing hill has been made with the soil from one of the ponds to allow visitors to look down on the design. Adjacent to the maze is an osier circle, 140 feet in diameter, consisting of seven concentric circles of different types of willows. Each type was selected for qualities of coloured bark and experiments with pruning give a variety of effects.

The fallen timber has been carefully cut to allow for large scale natural sculptures. Early designs included a pre-historic dinosaur an 'elephant howdah' and other eye-catching creations now appreciated by a growing number of visitors.

Ben's work will take many years to complete; appropriately it was started in 1988—then the European Year of the Environment (EYE).

Resurrection in Trimley

METHODISM in the village of Trimley was not very strong. The draughty old chapel had failed to attract the new families and in the summer of 1987 circuit representatives held an emergency meeting to discuss the future of Methodism in the area.

The storm, it seemed, solved the problem. Trimley Methodist Chapel was blown asunder; almost all the roof and half the walls were destroyed. Girders, masonry and rubble were scattered across the road and what was left of this sad chapel had to be quickly demolished. The chairman of the Ipswich circuit, the Rev Dr Richard Jones was left with 12 members and no chapel.

All seemed lost but the Methodist Insurance Company agreed, somewhat surprisingly, to provide a new chapel and new contents. A building in modern red brick, designed for today's needs, was built on the site. With a permanent sanctuary seating 50 people the new chapel was given many splendid features including sliding doors to increase seating capacity and a coffee bar and lounge.

Methodism in Trimley was revived; in fact the Methodist Recorder says the village has experienced a resurrection and the new premises was soon burgeoning with life, many local groups taking regular meetings in the chapel.

The opening service was conducted by the Rev Patrick McClusky, minister of the Felixstowe churches and the sermon preached by the Rev Malcolm Clark, superintendent of the Ipswich circuit. Other Methodist Churches in the Felixstowe area got together to donate a vivid stained glass window—with a central cross surrounded by Pentecostal flames and a dove of peace.

It was the dove that bore the olive branch when Noah's storm receded. This one has become a peaceful symbol of another great storm.

A collapsed hide on Havergate Island see p. 74.

Photograph by John Partridge

Photograph by East Anglian Daily Times

The Rev Patrick McClusky and in the background, the resurrection at Trimley.

Photograph by Chris Dunn

Willow trees between Bungay and Beccles—but not the quality for cricket bats.

Cricket—another crisis

ENGLISH cricket has faced many problems in recent years but the storm provided a different type of crisis—a shortage of quality cricket bats caused by the large number of storm-damaged willow trees. Thousands of willows fell in plantations in Suffolk and Essex, many of them before they had matured to the quality required.

The managing director of a Bungay company which specialises in growing and preparing timber for cricket bats said after the storm that there were enough willows lying on the ground to provide a 12-month supply, if no more were felled. After that the situation will begin to get grim and in five years time it could be serious.

The willows grown by Edgar Watts Ltd make bats for Test cricketers throughout the world so the problem is not just an English one.

Flatford Bridge earlier this century.

Photographs by Sandra Tricker, Suffolk County Council

Striking changes in evidence at Flatford Mill Bridge; Willy Lott's cottage is seen to the left of the pictures. Sandra Tricker is project officer for the Dedham Vale and Stour Valley countryside project, which assists in all areas of countryside appreciation, use and management and aims to enhance and conserve the landscape. Since the storm the interest of the general public in their work has increased markedly and there is a far greater awareness of the need for good landscape management.

Carol Carver remembers as she touches one of the young oaks planted in memory of her husband Bill. "They are planted in clumps in recognisable places, so we shall know they are Bill's trees. It is very peaceful with glimpses down to that lovely sweep of the river, and the birds sing their heads off. I think Bill would have approved."

Photograph by Simon Hodges, Forestry Commission

This aerial view of Rendlesham shows vividly the enormity of the damage with acre upon acre completely flattened.

An unusual view from the pulpit at Cransford Baptist Church, looking over farmland after the church was completely destroyed. The story of Cransford baptists was awaiting a happy outcome when in the summer of 1989 they were still using the village hall for services.

STORM WATERS
Looking out at 6.30 a.m. from his bedroom window at the Old Warehouse Chandlery, Oxford Quay, Hugh Bostock's picture captures the scene as small boats struggle for survival.

Photographs by Jan Michalak

Jan Michalak the head gardener at Ickworth, near Bury St. Edmunds fortuitously photographed the well known cedars from the roof of the house shortly before the storm, so their loss can be appreciated. In the replanting programme a technique for promoting deeper root growth has been employed. The young cedars have been planted on a small mound of earth; as their shallow roots spread sideways they meet the air and turn downwards thereby developing a much stronger root system. 200 new trees have been planted of which 70 are cedars.

Geoff Wheeler and his miller Simon in the workshop specially created for the purpose of building new sails and fan tail for Bardwell Windmill. See p.100

Photograph by Fern Flynn

Fritton Lake on the Somerleyton Estate, through which runs the North-eastern boundary of Norfolk and Suffolk. Together with many owners of large estates Lord Somerleyton suffered the loss of large numbers of mature trees and twenty-five acres of damaged woodland.

New Horizons—Thetford Forest bared.

Photograph by Fern Flynn

89

Fallen willows at Fye Bridge on the junction of Wensum Street and Magdalen Street in Norwich.

Photographs by Chris Dunn

Mousehold Heath Cottage Plantation and Valley Drive near Norwich. These before and after pictures show the damage caused by the storm and the opportunity for more imaginative replanting.

91

Picture: Duncan Morris

Waxham Great Barn seen from the Tower of Waxham Church, supported on all sides, July 1989, to prevent further collapse, its future hanging in the balance.

Photograph by Fern Flynn

Jomo the Leopard at Thrigby Hall Wildlife Park. A lucky cat. See story p. 113.

Photograph by: Fern Flynn

Derek Applegate, warden of the Horsey Windmill spent some hours climbing trees in order to see what fate had befallen this cherished landmark in North Norfolk. He arrived in time to see the wind lift off the fantail and send it crashing through the bridge which spans the nearby dyke. Derek also noticed that the rotating top of the windmill was lifting, and small craft nearby were already piled on top of each other. Damage was so great that the National Trust had to close the gallery to visitors for the next two summers but the idyllic appearance of the windmill has been restored.

Photograph by Bob Ogley

Beside the east gate leading to Heydon Church is a lime tree which fell in the great storm revealing the macabre sight of human bones as earth fell away from the roots. The unidentified bones were re-buried and the tree, after lopping tipped back into an enlarged hole. It is seen here in June 1989 thriving again—without bonemeal.

PRIVATE
NO
MOORING

Photograph by Duncan Morris

Hickling Broad. Small craft in extremis on the morning of October 16th, 1987.

Photograph by Chris Riggs

Photograph by Fern Flynn

A small miracle

St. Mary's Church in the village of Newbourne, near Ipswich, had for some time prior to October 1987 faced an uncertain future, unable to raise sufficient funds to justify its continued independent existence. Then came the storm.

After a funeral the previous day a careless hand had, perhaps, failed to close the old door firmly, and the great wind filled the church. Looking for a way out it behaved like a tornado hurling flowers into the rafters and prayerbooks all around turning their pages inwards, wrecking the altar and flinging a noticeboard from the wall against the organ. Enormous pressure built up within the church until a tremendous explosion was heard as the weakest spot gave way; the modern stained glass window in the east wall above the altar was blown out, broken into thousands of tiny pieces, soon to be covered by tons of rubble as the east wall itself collapsed on top of it. *Continued on following page*

Mrs. Judy Riggs, a regular worshipper, asked the workmen clearing the rubble to look particularly carefully in the debris for any broken fragments from the figure of Christ.

The next day a man appeared at her house next door carrying a piece of cloth. "Oh ma'am look what I've got you," he said unwrapping the head of Christ which he had found intact 6 feet deep under tons of rubble.

The incident has re-awoken the enthusiasm of villagers for their church; willing hands have appeared to help tidy the churchyard and elderly ladies have spent hours unfolding all the pages of the prayerbooks; although the insurance did not meet the cost of rebuilding, English Heritage, the Historic Churches Trust and the Suffolk Historic Churches Trust have all helped with donations; there only remains to be found £10,000 for the stained glass window but otherwise the future is bright for St. Mary's.

Photograph by: P. Holborn

The famous avenue of limes at Kentwell Hall, Long Melford have survived many violent gales including the great storm of 1703. Thanks to the initiative of tree surgeons they also survived the hurricane of 1987 but only because they were propped up after falling, pollarded and treated with the kind of respect reserved for really old soldiers. Like the welcoming avenue which is almost a mile long, the trees have a history running parallel to the history of this Elizabethan manor house, set in open parkland. The limes planted in 1678 by Sir John Robinson have become a symbol of resilience. In full summer leaf they are a wonderful sight. Our photograph above shows the fallen trees shortly after they were rescued, replanted and pollarded. Below is one rescued lime, wearing a magnificent new headdress in honour of its recreation. In the background is the Church of Long Melford.

Photograph by Fern Flynn

Parochial problems

The parish church of Thelnetham, which is close to the Suffolk/Norfolk border, felt the impact of the storm when three trees fell onto the roof, causing considerable damage. A fund was opened and the church roof (see picture below) was quickly repaired.

This experience was repeated in churchyards all over Suffolk. Leaning trees were removed, estimates obtained for repair and financial targets established. At Westhall, near Halesworth, however, there was a more delicate problem.

The cedar tree which fell against the 14th century chancel was enormous and access virtually impossible. Furthermore the parochial church council did not want to cause any more damage to the rare scissor brace construction and an appeal went out to parishioners asking for help.

For several weeks after the storm the tree remained in its lodging place while the council waited for the right people to turn up with the proper equipment. "We didn't dare to touch it", Mrs. Helen Holms told the Lowestoft Journal. "We asked a helicopter company if they could help but the tree, estimated to weigh 25 tons, was far too heavy."

As a result of the appeal Alistair Cameron came forward to tackle the task; with the help of equipment used on oil rigs, winches, turves, Mr. Cameron set up an arrangement of pulleys and successfully lifted it off. "It was in a particularly awkward position he said but eventually I managed it all right."

Another nearby church damaged was St. Mary's at Ditchingham. A seven foot pinnacle crashed from the tower through the roof of the nave. The Church was closed and the congregation worshipped at Hedenham or Broome. The pinnacle at Ditchingham is now back in place with its three companions. They are a distinctive feature of the Waveney Valley countryside.

Photograph by Eastern Daily Press

Three trees fell onto the roof of the parish church of Thelnetham close to the Suffolk/Norfolk border. The roof was badly damaged but many friends helped towards the fund to meet the cost of repair.

Photograph by Bob Ogley

Blickling Hall. Despite the ravages of the storm which brought down hundreds of trees and destroyed majestic avenues the staff worked feverishly to repair the damage and this jewel of Norfolk remains embowered in its sylvan setting. Below: Cattle in the Park with giant reminders of the storm.

Felbrigg Hall was cut off in the storm with many fallen trees across the long driveway. Here we see a new sapling replacing one of the fallen.

Photograph by East Anglian Daily Times   Photograph by Geoff Wheeler

The tragedy of Bardwell. Pictures taken directly after the storm.

Sailing into history

IMAGINE the wind blowing briskly in West Suffolk and the rotating tower of the Georgian windmill at Bardwell turning automatically so the great sails can catch the breeze. Imagine the driving power, the increasing momentum of the sails and then the smell of grinding corn. Imagine the miller down below, his hair whitened by flour, busy with the tools of his trade.

It sounds like a scenario from those halcyon days of long ago when Bardwell, like other Suffolk mills, was at the centre of a small family milling and wholefoods business.

The sails of Bardwell no longer turned but it was not age and dereliction which silenced them. It was wind—the wind which came from the direction of Bury on that disastrous morning of October 16, 1987. Like an ally turned foe this treacherous gale broke the windshaft, lifted the sails and sent them spinning through the air before crashing in the mill yard below.

A policeman and policewoman from the Suffolk Force, who had stopped outside the Bardwell Mill, watched the drama from just a few yards away and saw the sails leave the mill and fall on top of another 'old timer', the traction engine, Oliver. The owner of the mill, Geoffrey Wheeler, who was standing nearby put his arms around them and said: 'That's the end of a dream.'

Mr Wheeler and his wife Enid were inconsolable. Bardwell was one of only two windmills in the country in full-time production. Stoneground flour was produced six days a week and the couple's wholefoods business was highly acclaimed. Business 'died' that morning along with the windmill and to add insult to injury there was extensive damage to Oliver.

Like the storm itself the Bardwell tragedy has passed into history. After exhaustive problems with insurance claims, Geoff and Enid's faith was restored by the generosity shown to them by friends and neighbours in the village. This gave them the incentive to search the country for a foundry capable of casting a two-ton windshaft which acts as a hub for the windmill sails. It was not easy. An engineering job of this description had not been completed in England for more than 100 years.

By coming to the rescue Thurton Foundries in Norfolk added its name to the history books. Scale drawings and wooden patterns were made and then molten metal poured into the specially-prepared casts. The shaft was sent away for machining before being returned to Bardwell for installation.

Mr Wheeler then built a workshop and with his miller, Simon Wooster, made the new sails. Oliver has also been restored and he can provide the driving power, enabling Bardwell to continue its working life. See page 87.

Photograph by Brian Bedwell

It looks peaceful enough but a close inspection will show the Beccles town sign has been blown away and the wood facing the roundabout on the Bungay Road is a mass of fallen trees. In the centre of Beccles the roof of D. R. Grey, the opticians, was torn off by the wind and the town itself cut off by fallen trees. Picture below shows the famous sign back in place.

Photograph by F. Flunn

Photograph by Fern Flynn

At Southwold's Sutherland House Restaurant Mr. and Mrs. Wiggins were awoken at 3 a.m. by the sound of the wind carrying their sign clattering away down the street. Suddenly the end gable wall crashed into the yard of the Southwold Arms public house next door and then with a roar the dividing wall collapsed. The exposed roof cavity now acted like a funnel for the wind which swept through lifting the remaining tiles. Finally a picturesque and rare weeping ash in the small garden fell. Mr. and Mrs. Wiggins spent the rest of the night in the shelter of their garden studio. The historic old house which features an ornamental plaster ceiling has been repaired and with the help of a tree surgeon the ash restored to its position to delight the clientele.

Photograph by P. Norman

The trees that lined the Bury Road and fanned out across the
Suffolk/Cambridge border marked the attractive approach to the town of
Newmarket. Today they have virtually gone, victims of the storm and,
because of the dangerous state of those that remained, the woodman's axe.
The B1506 between Bury toll and the The Boy's Grave near Kentford was
closed for 3 weeks.

Photograph by Vernon Place

John Gardiner (centre) and friends on the road to Butley.

Photograph by Holly Pelling

No leaning trees, no devastation—the same spot today.

He gritted his teeth and clicked . . .

JOHN Gardiner, a British Telecom engineer, his wife Angie and two children live in a thatched cottage on the edge of the Tunstall Forest. surrounded by trees, mainly coniferous, the cottage looks more like a painting from a storybook. Rustic Lodge is close to Sudbourne Hall, a large house, whose one-time owner made himself an everlasting reputation by 'breaking the bank of Monte Carlo'.

That story has been well documented and, as far as John is concerned, is a tame everyday tale compared with the dramatic events which occurred around Rustic Lodge at dawn on Friday October 16, 1987.

John and Angie were awoken by the wind. The tall trees including a Redwood giant were swaying alarmingly. Branches were being snap-ped off and scattered goodness knows where. In the first light of dawn, John wisely took his family downstairs, and perhaps unwisely, ventured with his camera into the teeth of the gale.

John noticed a tree was about to fall on his house. Unable to do anything but watch the impending diaster, John pointed his camera towards the point of impact and gritted his teeth as he heard the tree crack and the accompanying echo fade into the forest. With a peculiar sense of satisfaction that at least he was recording a moment of personal drama, John clicked. Nothing happened—he had forgotten to open the lens shutter!

The tree had fallen and was resting against the thatch. John opened the shutter and took another picture and then, running round the garden, dodging trees as they fell, he finally recorded history as it was happening.

The angry sea. Storm whipped waves on the morning of the storm. Lowestoft Promenade seen from the Pier.

Photograph by Eastern Daily Press

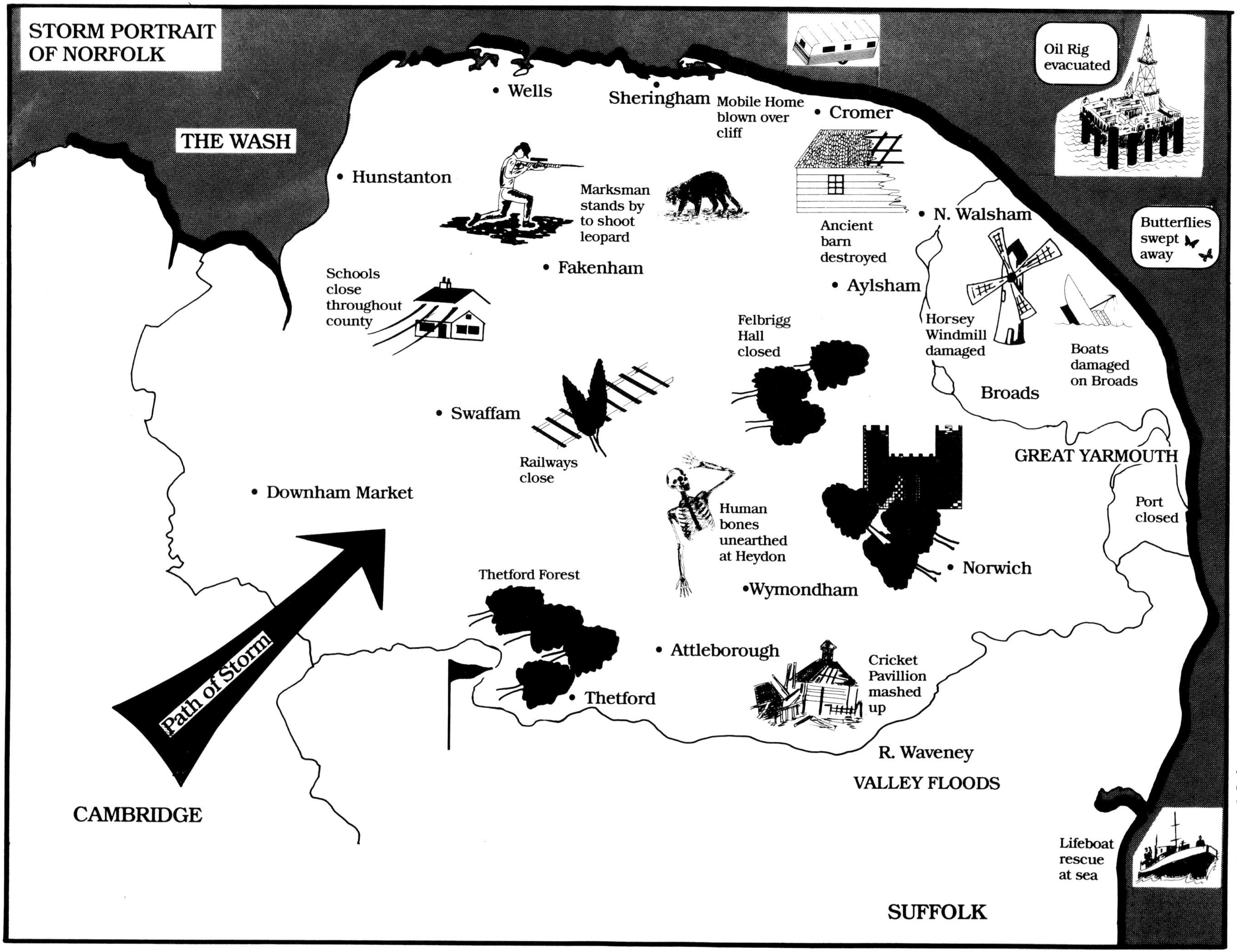

STORM PORTRAIT OF NORFOLK

THE WASH

Oil Rig evacuated

• Wells

Sheringham

Mobile Home blown over cliff

• Cromer

• Hunstanton

Marksman stands by to shoot leopard

Butterflies swept away

• N. Walsham

Ancient barn destroyed

• Fakenham

• Aylsham

Schools close throughout county

Felbrigg Hall closed

Horsey Windmill damaged

Boats damaged on Broads

Broads

• Swaffam

GREAT YARMOUTH

Railways close

Human bones unearthed at Heydon

Port closed

• Downham Market

•Wymondham

• Norwich

Thetford Forest

• Attleborough

Cricket Pavillion mashed up

• Thetford

R. Waveney

VALLEY FLOODS

Path of Storm

CAMBRIDGE

Lifeboat rescue at sea

SUFFOLK

Drawn by Pen and Ink

Still rising in Norfolk

NORFOLK is almost all man made. Gentle contours have become more gentle under the plough, the rivers have been diverted to flow in prescribed channels, trees have been planted and controlled and even the Broads have been created, if unintentionally, by the work of man.

Although the heyday of the country estate has passed there are many great mansions dotted all over the county. Sandringham, of course, Blickling, Felbrigg, Holkham and Sheringham all with impressive tree-lined avenues and colourful gardens. There are a large number of arable fields and a vast network of roads which provide access to every corner of the county.

There is nothing spectacular about Norfolk. No mountains or ridges or rocks to climb. The coast has no inlets and the only estuary is that at Great Yarmouth. Norfolk, however, has depth of beauty that is more subtle than that in most counties. It is an inspirational beauty which attracts artists, writers, poets and lovers of the countryside. The salt marshes, now under the protection of the National Trust, are visited frequently by bird watchers, the cliffs near Cromer are lofty and imposing and the great forests of Breckland could hide an entire army.

Norfolk is surrounded on three sides by the sea and has the widest variation of temperature of anywhere in England. There is nothing between north Norfolk and the North Pole and when the wind is in the east it can be bitingly cold.

It wasn't the east wind that caused havoc in Norfolk on the morning of October 16, 1987. The trouble came with a jet of warm air drawing behind it a wake of colder air from the north and west. As the wind in the south began to lose some of its intensity, the gale streamed out across Suffolk, Cambridge and into Norfolk. Still rising it careered on, over the Wash and into the vast blackness of the North Sea.

The Met men were astonished when they saw the statistics from the weather station at Gorleston. It showed a gust reading of 122 mph, the highest recorded anywhere on the English mainland. Calculations quickly showed that it was statistically improbable that a gust of equal strength would recur there for at least 200 years. But was it accurate?

First reports from the Met Office confirmed that the figure was correct and Norfolk had experienced gusts stronger than any in the south and stronger than anything in recorded history.

Further investigations revealed that the reading was false. The anemometer, it was discovered, had been vandalised and the cups damaged. Gorleston lost its place at the top of the gust league and Shoreham in Sussex took the honours. It didn't really matter to the people of Norfolk. The storm was the most serious to hit the county since 1953 when the notorious east coast floods accounted for so many lives. Those floods were caused by winds which lifted the tides over the sea walls—eight feet higher than their normal level in many places. But that was a wind which came from the east.

As the '87 storm crossed the border into Norfolk the Thetford Forest was the first point of resistance but the maelstrom of the wind tore through the forest with devastating force. It moved on to attack the great gardens and other woodlands where trees in full leaf, like the sails of tea clippers with roots sodden after many days of rain, began to topple.

In Norfolk, as in parts of Essex and Suffolk, the first thrust of the storm brought heavy rain with it and there was flooding in many river valleys, made worse by fallen trees which blocked the rivers. Anglian Water called in extra teams to clear a four mile stretch of the Wensum Valley where the Taverham to Costessey road was flooded.

Thetford suffered badly and an early estimate suggested 20,000 cubic metres of forest has been wiped out. The National Trust did not escape. Blickling Hall had to be closed immediately for tree clearance. Felbrigg lost many fine specimens and Sheringham, on the north coast, lost 250 trees before the storm vanished into the turbulent waste.

It is a wild, restless sea which washes the coast of Norfolk, shallower than most, saltier and dangerous. But the sea that laps along the shore is usually driven by the 'Norseman's Wind'—rarely do such ferocious gales come from the direction of Suffolk.

On these shores brawny lifeboatmen and coastguards prepared for the worst but it was a more delicate species that perished at Yarmouth. The Butterfly Centre had large sections of the roof and walls blown out and 200 rare butterflies and 30 birds were swept away.

At sea there was no lack of drama. Forty rig workers had to be airlifted from a gas rig off Cromer as a stricken vessel drifted dangerously close. Lifeboatmen braved appalling seas off Lowestoft to go to the aid of a British coaster. Vessels were warned not to enter Yarmouth harbour where coastguards reported Force 11 winds.

Prompt action by fish farmers at Dereham saved 500 carp and catfish when the storm cut off life-sustaining oxygen supplies to their tankers. Tragically, farmer Sidney Riches died in his wrecked car at Tottenhill after collision with a lorry at a point where the A10 was blocked by fallen trees.

Why didn't the Met Men warn us, was the cry in Norfolk as county and district councils held crisis talks to assess the damage. The leader of NCC and MP's throughout the county supported the need for financial help from the Government.

Aid came to this great county in the form of Government money and, more important, individual help. Gardeners, farmers, foresters, fishermen, firemen, council workers, telephone and water engineers, soldiers, traders, electricians, railwaymen, voluntary workers and neighbours all played their part in the great recovery.

Castle Mound, Norwich on the morning of the storm.

Photograph by Eastern Daily Press

Thetford handicaps

Photograph by Eastern Daily Press

THETFORD golfers, whether members or visitors, have always been influenced by the magical setting of the course and its remoteness from the world beyond. Here the forest was like a companion—an inspiration to enjoy a great game, whatever the season.

However, sad days fell upon this happy club. The first was the decision to cut the course in two for the much-needed Thetford by-pass. After long negotiations with the Forestry Commission new greens and fairways were introduced between the tall trees.

It was a happy compromise until the storm. Uprooted pines and forest debris littered the new fairways and our photograph of golf professional Norman Arthur illustrates the desperation of the situation.

The broken trees and stumps have been removed and as a new growth takes hold, Thetford golfers are smiling again. Tranquillity (see below) is returning fast, but no one has been able to prevent the tarmac scar through the forest—introduced in the name of progress.

Photograph by Fern Flynn

After the clearance and replanting the peacefulness returns

Photograph by Eastern Daily Press

A view of The Street, Cantley from an electricity board helicopter.

Electricity

EASTERN Electricity took full-page advertisements in newspapers throughout East Anglia to show that their rescue armies were in the field. 'We're Working Flat Out', screamed the title. 'Since dawn on that fateful day we've been working 24 hours a day, restoring power to customers. And as you can imagine coping with the worst storm since records began isn't easy. We've flown in crews from all over the country to help speed up repairs. Please be patient. We're trying our hardest.'

So they were. One in four of Eastern Electricity's 2¾ million customers were without power, more than 300 staff were working day and night and reinforcement teams were flown in from Scotland and Northern Ireland. A fleet of helicopters carried engineers to inaccessible damage and vital repair equipment was lowered in from the air.

The final repair bill for Eastern Electricity was massive but work continued on faulty equipment long after most consumers had been reconnected. For the men in the field it was a long, hard, exhausting job but as one of them said—'there was light at the end of the tunnel'.

Photograph by Eastern Daily Press

Sad story of the Waxham Barn

IF the storm had totally demolished the Waxham medieval barn, one of the most valuable 16th century thatched buildings in England, then a long-running local controversy would have been tragically resolved.

The barn, near Winterton, just yards from the sea, was merely mutilated causing even greater anxiety to English Heritage and Norfolk County Council, whose plans to restore it and open it to visitors were now completely shattered.

Farmer Henry Harvey, who has struggled for many years with the Herculean task of maintaining the barn, has lived at Waxham all his life. The barn forms part of the 16th century farm complex and only the purpose-built cattle sheds and a Georgian addition to the house detracts from a genuine Tudor farm.

There are no lack of gale-force winds in this bleak corner of Norfolk but Henry and his son Henry jnr soon realised that the wind which was whipping pieces of thatch over the sea wall sounded rather more menacing than usual. They saw the roof of the barn lifting and, risking obvious danger, opened the doors and led 20 Ayreshire cows to the comparative safety of a more modern structure.

By this time the plastic covering protecting the ancient timbers was billowing and the wind was trapped inside. The eastern end of the barn collapsed, part of the roof caved in and timber and masonry were sent cartwheeling across the farm with the plastic dragging behind.

When the storm passed the Harveys saw that their invaluable, almost priceless, medieval showpiece was in ruins. Meetings which had been held between the Harveys, the county council, English Heritage and the local MP before the storm, now seemed to be invalidated. Questions were asked. Could the barn be saved? Who would pay the repair bill, now double that of the original estimate for restoration? Were the Harveys to blame for opening the barn doors to save their stock? Should the county go ahead with its plans to compulsorily purchase the building?

Henry and Mary Harvey, aggravated by what had become a long drawn out and unpleasant saga, had their own answer. Saddened that the storm had not completed the job they applied for a demolition order.

The Waxham controversy continues.

See page 92

Butterflies thrive again

THE Butterfly Centre at Great Yarmouth was designed to survive extreme weather conditions and actually stood up well to winds which gusted at almost 100 mph. Unfortunately seaside paraphernalia on the pier was not so resilient and the butterfly house was bombarded with flying objects, one of which crashed through the roof—followed by the wind.

Half the roof was lifted off and butterflies and birds were swept away. The entire stock was killed except for three caged birds—and these were stolen by looters while the wind was still blowing.

Mike and Doreen Turner who own the Butterfly Centre were understandably upset. They had spent two years in creating a tropical oasis that had become one of the greatest attractions in Yarmouth. A living display of exotic butterflies fluttered in the humidity of this seafront greenhouse feeding on an abundance of flowering plants. More than 100 species thrived in these conditions.

The Turners were depressed but not defeated. They set to work on reconstructing the centre with a completely new design. Within a week the glass roof had been replaced. Bridges and waterfalls were created, the ponds were reconstructed, tropical plants grown and an entire new stock of birds and butterflies introduced including the very rare South American Zebra (Heliconius charitonius). The Centre today is as popular as ever and the Turners are delighted with the re-creation.

Photograph by Eastern Daily Press

Andrew Raine, a member of staff in the battered Butterfly Centre.

Photograph by Fern Flynn

Mike Turner in a new, and better, butterfly farm.

Jomo is spared

JOMO is a spotted leopard presented to Thrigby Hall Wildlife Gardens by Chester Zoo in 1979. He has fathered many cubs and is one of Thrigby's great personalities.

On the morning of the storm Jomo's life was in the balance. Police marksmen stood by with rifles poised fearing that the wind would set up a getaway route for Jomo into the Norfolk countryside. But the Tree of Heaven, which grew from the centre of his cage, remained intact and Jomo's long life was spared.

The drama at Thrigby unfolded as the winds grew in intensity. Specimen trees in the wildlife gardens fell and director Mrs Beryl Sims was woken by the noise. Although Jomo's cage is designed to crumple rather than split, her main concern was that the tree would fall and smash open the compound. "Leopards usually avoid humans but I didn't want to take any risks," she said.

Mrs Sims called for a veterinary surgeon and they were joined by the two girl keepers, Linda Barnes and Sharon Stafford. The vet considered tranquillising Jomo but was worried that an air-born dart, would not hit its target in the prevailing wind so eventually called the police and three marksmen arrived from Norwich.

Meanwhile Mrs Sims' husband, Kenneth was on a zoo tour in Germany unaware of the problems at Thrigby until a colleague told him there had been a "bit of a blow in England but all was OK now." The coach driver having heard more news was less tactful. "The police are shooting your leopard. They are scared stiff."

When Mr Sims arrived home he found that Jomo had been safely moved out of the danger area and the staff had behaved admirably in the most harrowing conditions.

Despite his great age Jomo was none the worse for his ordeal and today he is as sprightly as ever. So is Xiang, a clouded leopard, who was transferred to Thrigby from Howletts Zoo near Canterbury sometime after the storm. Xiang has a different tale because he actually escaped in the night and spent a week roaming around the devastated Kent countryside before he was enticed back with meat. The photograph shows Xiang at the delightful moment he was reunited with his keeper. (See also page 93)

A gift is carved

TYRREL'S wood, near Pulham Market is today the scene of great activity as work continues to extract the giant 200-year-old oak trees which toppled so dramatically.

The wood is owned by The Woodland Trust, one of 370 in such ownership across the country and, arguably, received the most damage although the new vegetation is growing so fast that only those who knew Tyrrel's Wood prior to October 1987 would notice the complete change of character.

Trust members who mourned the loss of this ancient woodland have received a small memento in the form of gifts of wood which have been carved from the fallen oak trees.

Regional Officer, Julian Rowton, who is responsible for 45 woods in East Anglia explained how difficult it was to extract heavy wood from a wet area with rather hazardous obstacles without causing too much rutting. Much of the further end of the 41-acre wood had not been touched.

He also explained how a large corrugated iron building had been plucked by the wind and thrown to a new site 50 yards away. It collapsed on impact and the Territorial Army were called in to demolish it.

Mr Rowton is replanting with oak, hornbeam, hazel, rowan, maple and alder and attempting to control the sycamore which threatens to take over.

Xiang—pleased to be home.

Photograph by N. Hollist, Mail Newspapers

Photograph by Eastern Daily Press

When Bill and Joan Last moved into their bungalow at Poringland in 1977 they were surrounded by oak trees. Fearing they might crash on their home in a storm the couple asked South Norfolk District Council to prune or take them down. Officials agreed to fell six trees but claimed the remaining five, which carried preservation orders, were safe. The storm proved a point in the most terrifying way. One oak tree fell on the Last's garage, flattening the family car and four motor cycles. The second missed the living room by inches. Bill and Joan and their 22-year-old son Kevin had no desire to wait for the third. They fled for their lives. The family had been involved in a long argument over the safety of the trees. Joan said: "It was nasty and frightening. We just evacuated the place as quickly as possible." Feeling they should be compensated the Last's considered taking the council to court, but were unable to proceed with their case because they had no written evidence that the trees were unsafe, prior to the storm. The two remaining trees were removed by the council—for safety. Picture shows Kevin with the demolished garage.

Photograph by Eastern Daily Press

The roof of Victoria Lodge Guest House, Nelson Road South, Great Yarmouth, showing the hole made when the chimney crashed through the roof into the kitchen, where, only seconds earlier, Mrs. Pat Shepherd had been preparing breakfast.

Photograph by Eastern Daily Press

Photograph by Ceinwen Thomas

The children of Norfolk, as in other counties, will never forget the day of the storm. Those who actually managed to get to school found themselves clearing debris from school grounds in place of lessons and, of course, many schools were badly damaged and the children sent home. A large tree fell on Thetford's Norwich Road First and Middle School and the picture (above left) shows two men battling with the branches. At Norwich, Blackdale Middle School on Bluebell Road was closed while a tree was removed from a classroom. Forty trees also fell in the school grounds and a nearby wood and after the clearing up Blackdale children were encouraged to replant. The storm was certainly an adventure and the days that followed provided an education in environmental care. Picture shows Joanna Williams and Tracy O'Donovan planting a sapling helped by Ian Tunnicliff from the British Trust of Conservation Volunteers.

A splendid knock

FOR many years members of Old Buckenham Cricket Club looked at the tatty, prefabricated wooden buildings which served as changing rooms and vowed to demolish them. In their place they would build a brick pavilion more in keeping with their famous ground.

On October 16, just two weeks after the end of the successful summer season of 1987, half the work was done for them. Like a villainous hero the storm appeared out of nowhere and paused briefly at Old Buckenham near Attleborough where it took a liking to the great trees encircling the cricket ground. The wind then picked up the old wooden buildings and smashed them to matchwood. It was the kind of demolition job that members themselves had promised but never started. Now they had to rebuild.

Naturally they were fully insured with the Norwich Union, sponsors of their Norwich Alliance cricket league, who looked kindly upon this pavilionless storm-ravaged club. Chairman Chris Allen and secretary Harry Plank encouraged members to raise additional funds and from the ashes rose a magnificent clubhouse complete with bar, where they toasted the wind.

Ashes is an appropriate word in Old Buckenham for an unofficial Test Match between England and Australia was played there in 1921 when Warwick Armstrong and his all-conquering Aussies took on Jack Hobbs, Percy Fender et al. The teams changed in a marvellous pavilion of Norfolk thatch which was eventually taken away from Old Buckenham—not by the wind but the owners of the nearby hall. It stands today in the grounds of a school in another county.

So Old Buckenham with its lush, flat square of quality turf looks kindly upon this October wind which blew a little good to one of the country's most picturesque cricket grounds.

Photograph by Buckenham Cricket Club

The old pavilion wrecked and, below, a gift of the storm.

Photograph by Fern Flynn

Photograph by Eastern Daily Press

River officers issued urgent warnings to holidaymakers and boat owners on the day of the storm. "Don't go out on the Broads, fallen trees have been washed away by the current and some may be floating just below the surface." The Yarmouth Port and Haven Commissioners said it was impossible for boats to pass under many bridges because of exceptionally high water levels. Some owners would have liked the opportunity to move on but, sadly, their boats had capsized in the storm and many had sunk. Many holidaymakers abandoned their houseboats and one couple at Hickling Broad who escaped from their disintegrating gas-filled boat say they are lucky to be alive. The photograph taken on the day of the storm looks serene enough but the water level was high and danger lurked below the surface.

Photograph by Joyce Middleton

Photograph by Chris Dunn

A falling tree in Tombland, Norwich flattened a bus shelter and lifted electric cables out of the ground. The site has been restored and inset picture shows the then Lord Mayor of Norwich, Gary Wheatley planting a replacement tree.

Photographs by Eastern Daily Press

This brick wall at the rear of the Idears shop in Diss fell over with a tremendous wallop and, in tribute to the skill of the bricklayer, remained almost intact. The town was badly hit by the storm which actually occurred on market day. This was abandoned, stallholders deciding against setting up their stalls when many of the roads into Diss were blocked by fallen trees.

The Taverham to Costessey Road was underwater after the River Wensum burst its banks and our picture shows a lorry carefully negotiating the rising floods. A four-mile stretch along the Wensum was flooded and Anglian Water teams were brought in to clear fallen trees blocking the river.

Photograph by Eastern Daily Press

As the gale careered into the North Sea between Cromer and The Wash it had one final sting in its tail—and that was enough to sweep a mobile home from the Seaview Caravan Park at East Runton over the cliff edge and onto the beach below. Fortunately the home was not occupied but it was totally demolished and its contents scattered all over the sand. The young 'retrievers' above returned to the site with many armfuls of personal belongings.

Hero of the night

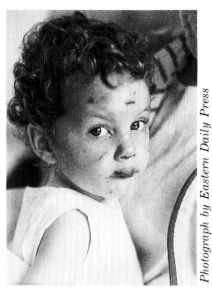

Photograph by Eastern Daily Press

IN this short pictorial history of the Great Storm in the Eastern counties there are many tales of courage, resolution and independence and they shine through page after page. The rescue armies in the field who battled against impossible odds, the lifeboatmen who set out in hurricane force winds, the foresters and gardeners who never gave up and, of course, the neighbours who showed and are still showing great kindness. There are many others.

We have found a special hero with which to close this chapter on Norfolk. A healthy, happy five year old red-headed boy whose smiling face today shows no sign of a harrowing ordeal in the early hours of *that* morning.

Matthew Nuttall was buried alive when the chimney of his grandparents' home collapsed sending part of the roof crashing down on top of him. In just a couple of seconds Matthew was completely covered with plaster, rubble, debris and dust.

His grandparents, Peter and Colleen High of Beccles Road, Bradwell had to use their bare hands to pull away the debris. Beneath it they found the bruised and bleeding face of a confused and shocked three-year old whose terrifying experience was destined to live with him for a long, long time.

Matthew was taken to James Paget Hospital, Gorleston for treatment for his injuries and for shock. Psychologically the latter could have been more serious than the many cuts and bruises on Matthew's face and body.

He was staying with his grandparents because his mother and father, Steven and Mandy Nuttall of Hamilton Road, Yarmouth had won a holiday to France. The holiday was cancelled and the Nuttalls returned to the drama back home.

The photograph of Matthew today shows that the facial scars have healed and, as far as that nightmare event is concerned, it was several adventures into the past.

Those who are close to him will never forget the night and they will never forget the courage of a little miracle boy who clawed his way free helped by two frantic but greatly relieved grandparents.

Photograph by Claire Ogley

Was the storm really such a bad thing?

by Dr. Oliver Rackham, who tutors in the Botany Department at Cambridge and is a research fellow at Corpus Christi College. Dr. Rackham is an acknowledged authority on the English landscape and his book The History of the Countryside, published in 1986 is the most authoritative and up-to-date work available.

AS anyone can see from the pictures, most of the spectacular damage was in streets, gardens and forestry plantations: wild trees in wood and hedgerow suffered relatively less. Most affected were young trees that had recently reached full size: they had developed maximum windage but not the massive stems and roots which might have withstood the gale. Least affected were ancient and historic trees like the Culford Oak or the Haughley Oak. For example, in Rendlesham Forest, several square miles of giant young pines, some 50 years old, were snapped off or uprooted almost to a tree (p.72). In their midst are the 4,000 medieval pollard oaks of Staverton Park, among the most wonderful ancient oaks in England, of which barely a score were overturned.

Few of the trees 'lost' in the storm were actually killed. Most trees, of course, regenerate broken limbs or tops as they do after pollarding; it was surprising to find that they cope with uprooting too. A great majority of uprooted deciduous trees, where not interfered with, are still alive, and most of them flourish horizontally; this includes about half the ancient oaks uprooted in Staverton. Even conifers, which are more set in their ways, have survived uprooting more often than not.

The storm itself was not an ecological tragedy. Most affected were planted trees, which are replaceable and are not part of our wildlife. In forestry plantations they would have been felled anyway in a few years. The Forestry Commission has successfully retrieved and stored the timber from Rendlesham, and has not lost much of its value. Hybrid poplars, snapped or uprooted all over East Anglia, would have been felled already (on reaching forty years old) had the market for which they had been planted still existed.

The storm spared virtually all the irreplaceable trees and woods—ancient woods and ancient trees, which are of supreme value as a habitat as well as for their historical meaning. No ancient wood was irrevocably damaged by the storm. Coppice stools have sometimes been uprooted, as at Chalkney Wood (Essex), but have stayed alive and will go back into their holes at the next coppicing. As a habitat, a horizontal tree—alive or dead—is at least as good as a vertical one. The uprooting has often revived woodland plants that had been waiting as buried seed for forty years and more since the wood was last felled.

In itself the storm was a bonus for woodland conservation; not so the public's or the official reaction to it. It was at once assumed—without waiting until the effects could be known—that the storm was a tragedy, and that money would put it right. Trees had failed to conform to their masters' ideas of what a tree is and how it should behave, and must be put in their place. Dangerously large amounts of money had suddenly to be spent on meeting a unique situation that was not fully understood.

All through that very wet winter, machines galumphed through woods removing fallen trees, to be sold at bottom prices. On the land thus cleared, trees were got from somewhere and hastily stuck in the ground. Clearing and replanting have already killed many more trees, and done more damage to woodland, than the storm itself.

Where the trees blown down were themselves known to have been planted, replanting was, maybe, the right course of action, though even here there should have been a pause for thought. Planted trees almost certainly fared disproportionately worse in the storm than wild ones. To replant risks setting up the same circumstances—a landscape of big, young, poorly-rooted trees—in which the same consequences will be repeated when there is a high wind in, say, sixty years' time. Many planted trees are in the wrong places. What happened to the beeches around Newmarket (p.103) is one of the uprootings that happen there every few years; beech is not native to these thin chalk soils and does not root well on them.

In East Anglia and Essex, wiser counsels prevailed, and less damage was done by reckless replanting than in south-east England. Rochford District Council is responsible for many of the public and historic woods in S.E. Essex, where the storm's effects were particularly spectacular (p.37) but virtually no trees were killed. The Council decided to do little but what was necessary to prevent loose boughs from falling on people's heads. They were not to be deflected from their well-considered coppicing programme. They published a leaflet to explain why replanting was unnecessary and how the woods would rapidly sort themselves out.

By the time these words appear, two years will have elapsed. An attempt will have been made to restore most formal landscapes, but is is one thing to plant trees, and another to keep them alive. Many ancient woods and wild trees will have been left more or less to themselves. Landowners who have done this should not be reproached nor prodded into 'doing something positive', even at this late stage. In two years the problems have gone far towards solving themselves. To let well alone turns out to have been the best way of conserving natural woodland.

A record lost

THERE is little doubt that the Great Storm of October '87 has been more closely studied than any single weather event since Lynmouth in 1952 and the East Coast floods a year later. The Met office in failing to warn of the impending disaster received criticism so hostile that two committees were set up to investigate. They both concluded that much of the criticism was misplaced but recommended that important changes should be made in the way that information is gathered.

The anemometer at Gorleston.

Weather, the excellent monthly magazine published by the Royal Meteorological Society devoted its March 1988 issue to a close examination of all the features of the storm and referred particularly to the strength of the wind at Gorleston which recorded a gust of 122 mph. This incredible reading put the Gorleston weather station at the top of the British Isles league table and it was quoted in all official data reports including the Burt and Mansfield article in Weather.

When the anemograms were received at Bracknell just after the storm it was known that the Gorleston direction record was defective because the vane had been vandalised a month earlier. Subsequently it was discovered that the anemometer cups were also damaged and were bent downwards by 90 degrees. The anemometer head was removed and sent to the Operational Instrumention Branch at the Met. Office, where tests in the wind tunnel showed that the speed was over-registering by about 20 per cent at most levels.

Gorleston lost its place at the top and there was revised thinking about the strength of the wind over Norfolk and particularly this part of the North Sea. Sussex suffered stronger winds after all and the value of more than 113 mph at Shoreham-by-Sea was accepted as the maximum observed gust in the British Isles, though the exact time remains unknown because of the power failure.

Although the gusts touched hurricane force the storm was not a true hurricane in the way that Gilbert of Jamaica undoubtedly was. However, this technicality has not invalidated the widely held belief that this was the nearest thing Britain is going to have to a full-blown hurricane.

Stormy weather

by Norman Brooks
a fellow of the Royal Meteorological Society

FOR those living in Essex and East Anglia there was nothing particularly noteworthy about the rather sullen autumnal weather on October 15, 1987, and apart from the now-legendary comment by Michael Fish on BBC TV at lunchtime, there was little to denote the presence of any impending storm.

Few people heard the late evening warnings of high winds, so those in the easternmost parts of the region were totally unprepared for the devastation that was to greet them at dawn.

The abiding memory of most will be the unfamiliar, almost alien, shriek of the wind, and the utter fury of the gusts that made even the walls of sturdily built homes shake.

In the gathering light, the elemental struggle of trees fighting for their very existence came into view, with the ground heaving around their trunks as if in an ocean swell. The combination of saturated soil after weeks of wet weather, and a still-intact leaf burden, meant that many trees had a hopeless fight maintaining a 'hold' in the ground.

A few days after the storm it was noticeable that much tree foliage presented a scorched and dead appearance. It is most likely that this was caused by the rain, which fell during the storm, containing a high salt content picked up from the sea. The effect was not confined only to localities adjacent to the coast.

Meteorologically, the event was caused by a fast-moving and vigorous depression, fuelled by an exceptional temperature gradient of 10 deg C. By 0200 hours GMT on October 16 the pressure had fallen to 957 millibars near Exeter, making it the deepest depression to be centred over England and Wales for at least 150 years. Winds were already reaching gale force in the West Country and by 0400 hours GMT the storm had reached East Anglia.

At 0500 hours with the depression now centred between Leicester and Peterborough the wind reached its peak intensity in Norfolk, Suffolk and Essex, with a slow abatement in strength after 0800 hours GMT. The most severe winds were experienced to the south-east of the depression, along the coasted margins of east-Norfolk east-Suffolk and most of Essex, with a wind speed of 40-50 kt (severe gale and storm force) and gusts in excess of 70 kt at the height of the storm.

The highest gusts in the East were 87 kt (100 mph) at Shoeburyness and 78 kt at Hemsby, both hurricane force on the Beaufort scale.

The storm of 1987 has been compared to many, most notably to that of November 26/27, 1703, so graphically described by Daniel Defoe. A direct comparison, for obvious reasons is difficult.

Great storms in the east

September 1895: Great Waltham suffered a storm of 'unprecedented fury' in the early hours of September 7 when a tornado struck. The village magazine tells how 'Scarcely a roof kept out the deluge of water and the stoutest of houses seemed fairly to reel under the shock. As the storm neared it seems to have taken the form of a whirlwind. For 20 minutes beforehand the roar was heard, and in scarcely more than 10 minutes it had spent its force—but what a ten minutes it was!'

June 1897: Chelmsford and its surrounding villages were bombarded by hailstones 'as big as walnuts' in a sudden storm which wrought havoc to mid-Essex on Thursday June 24. Storm clouds began to gather in the early afternoon and the temperature rose to a stifling 88° fahrenheit. By 2.45 the sky had become a mixture of ink and fused copper, and it was so dark that gas lamps had to be lit in offices, shops and factories. 'Immediately the storm began,' says a contemporary report, 'a scene was presented that has no parallel in local memory.' Rain fell in torrents and hailstones 'literally shot out of the clouds'. In Ingatestone lumps of hail were said to be larger than hens' eggs, and a man in charge of a horse and cart had his cheek cut open by a jagged piece of ice.

February 1953: A storm surge driven by ferocious north-westerly winds crashed against the East Coast sea defences in what was one of the most infamous and certainly most tragic weather events in East Anglia this century. In the north channel the motor vessel Princes Victoria sank with the loss of 132 lives. At King's Lynn the predicted tide was 6.6 metres (21.6 feet) but the water came up two metres higher.

The town centre was flooded by a wave. No one knew the flood water was coming as the noise it made was muffled by the roaring gale. All along the eastern coastline the sea wall was breached and on the Essex shore most of Canvey Island's 12,000 people were evacuated. 156 people lost their lives in the counties of Essex, Norfolk, Suffolk and Lincolnshire.

September 1958: A highly-charged electrical storm brought its own fury to mid-Essex one extremely hot and sultry afternoon in early September. As in the storm of 1897 hailstones mingled with torrential rain that fell non-stop from mid-afternoon until the early hours of the following morning. Ripe crops waiting to be harvested were ruined within minutes; tons of coke and phurnacite stacked outside the boiler room were washed onto the playing fields at Moulsham Secondary School in Chelmsford, while Ingatestone suffered its worst flooding in memory. More of the village would have been under water had not excavations for the long-awaited by-pass begun. The great trench, twenty-one feet deep in places, acted as a moat and saved many homes from the flood as it filled with water pouring in a river from Fryerning.

January 1976: After a week of stormy weather a depression moved across Scotland into the North Sea during the night of January 2/3, subsequently deepening and bringing severe gales with winds of hurricane force or more. Among high gusts were 105 mph at Wittering, 108 at Cromer, 102 at Norwich where every road out of the city was blocked by fallen trees. Structural damage was widespread and particularly severe in East Anglia. As with the storm of 1953 the depression produced a storm surge in the North Sea but the improved sea defences were only breached in a few places. Twenty four people died in Britain.

Photograph by Eastern Daily Press

An old lady is rescued from an upstairs room. This was the scene in Great Yarmouth during the East Coast floods of 1953.

Gale damage at Sandringham in February 1908 when hundreds of fine trees were destroyed.

February 2, 1953: The river Glaven at Cley-next-the sea in North Norfolk burst its banks as sea water forced it back inland. The river widened to ¼ mile in one spot bounded by the churches of Wiverton and Newgate.

Photograph by Eastern Daily Press

Photographs by Gordon Anckorn collection

February 5, 1924: The tide at King's Lynn was one of the highest for years. The water came 28 feet 5 inches above the dock sill and these buoys floated away from the Common Staithe Quay, along Ferry Street and within 90 yards of the Tuesday market.

Photograph courtesy of Orford Fun Day Committee

The scene at Orford, Suffolk in November 1963 outside the Jolly Sailor public house. Freak winds and a rainstorm of tropical intensity caused havoc in the village.

No pen could describe it, nor tongue express it, nor thought conceive it unless by one in the extremity of it.

Daniel Defoe on the Great Tempest of Nov 26, 1703

About the authors

Bob Ogley

Bob is the author of the book *In the Wake of The Hurricane* which covered the trail of the storm to hit southern England in October 1987. It became a national bestseller and remained in the top ten for eight consecutive months. It was highly acclaimed by critics all over the world.

He has just retired as editor of the Sevenoaks Chronicle, a weekly newspaper in Kent, where he has been deeply rooted for more than 25 years. Bob will now concentrate on his own publishing business which he established after his first book was rejected.

Encouraged by his series of hurricane books which includes the most ferocious storm of all time *Hurricane Gilbert*, Bob has teamed up with Kev Reynolds to produce this regional version for the eastern counties of England.

Kev Reynolds

Kev Reynolds is an Essex man, born in Ingatestone and educated at Moulsham Secondary School in Chelmsford. His first years of working life were spent in the county town before leaving to become a Youth Hostel warden.

After nearly 20 years in this work he turned to full-time writing. He is now a freelance writer, photographer and lecturer specialising in mountains and countryside topics.

This is Kev's 15th book.

128

Hurricane Books from Froglets

In the Wake of the Hurricane (Kent Edition)............ISBN 0-9513019-0-X.................£7.00
In the Wake of the Hurricane (National)....................ISBN 0-9513019-18...................£7.50
In the Wake of the Hurricane (Hardback)................ISBN 0-9513019-4-2................£11.95
Surrey in the Hurricane..ISBN 0-9513019-2-6.................£7.50
Hurricane Gilbert.. ISBN 0-9513019-5-0.................£7.50

"We chroniclers of the storm all stand in debt to Bob Ogley in much the same degree as all other epic poets stand in debt to Homer" **—George Hill, Hurricane Force.**

"It is indeed a remarkable record of a dreadful night and a record which will become part of the history of our country" **—Denis and Margaret Thatcher, 10 Downing Street.**

Literary fate has made him a star—something he declines being at his roots a countryman who has pumped his typewriter and cracked his staff into action over the past 18 years. Because of demand In the Wake of The Hurricane is more elusive than Spycatcher.
—Exeter Express and Echo.

As a record of the power of nature mocking the efforts of man and as a reminder of the vulnerability of things we take so much for granted this is an awesome volume.
—Kev Reynolds, Environment Now

Among writers, the patriarch and forerunner of all chroniclers of the storm is Bob Ogley, editor of the local paper in Sevenoaks, Kent. **—The Times.**

This first book on the hurricane adds flesh to the bones of the growing legend of the night of October 16, 1987. **—Express and Star, Wolverhampton.**

An album of reports and photographs of the devastation on a scale more familiar with the Far East and the Caribbean. Bob Ogley's sensational collection is a reminder of the need to restore as well as rebuild. **—The Guardian.**

Bob Ogley has captured the century's worst storm with this magnificent best selling book.
—Frank Thompson, Daily Mail.

What an inspired idea to cover the hurricane's trail. This really is a magnificent book.
—Group Capt Sir Leonard Cheshire VC

In the Wake of the Hurricane has a dramatic array of pictures, some of which were taken from a plane which Bob Ogley hired. He was especially well-placed to mourn the falling of Sevenoaks' eponymous trees. **—The Independent.**

Bob experienced every waking minute in the teeth of the storm and wrote a best seller, In the Wake of the Hurricane. He is an ardent conservationist—a man who has spent nearly all his life immersed in the countryside. **—Bob Bryant, Gloucester Citizen.**

A first class production and an excellent record of the devastation that hit our part of Kent on the night of October 16, 1987. Bob Ogley has put it together with great speed and commendable skill. **—Winston S Churchill, Westerham.**

Bob Ogley's bright idea for a book on the hurricane meant a victory over condescending publishers. **—Michael O'Flaherty, Daily Express.**

The success of his collection of vivid photographs and dramatic text was immediate; the book became number two in the paperback list. Sceptical publishers had given no encouragement. **—Rachel Warren, Evening Standard.**

The book has sold a staggering 90,000 copies in eight months, broken sales records in Kent, spent many weeks in the bestsellers lists and raised £40,000 for charity.**—Mike Swain, Today.**

This book is not all gloom and doom but an inspiration too, to visit many of the places illustrated.
—Doug Murphy, Surrey Mirror, Leatherhead.

Bob Ogley's text is charged with a caring local journalist's insight and feeling for the community. **—Frank Sellens, Courier Newspapers.**